YouTube

FOOTBALL FANTASTIC!

IAIN SPRAGG

CARLTON
BOOKS

CONTENTS

INTRODUCTION

Welcome to the only football book that lets you see all the goals, gaffes and incredible incidents for yourself. Enter the short URL or scan the QR code into your phone, tablet, laptop or computer and witness these amazing football moments in action.

Football is a funny old game and in *YouTube Football Fantastic!* we celebrate the comedy capers, hilarious blunders and touchline mishaps that make the world's favourite sport such a rib-tickling spectacle.

From the armed and dangerous Brazilian referee to the South African ball boy who was sent for an early bath, from the linesman who got on the wrong side of an angry bird to Spider-Man's surprise Premier League pitch invasion, *YouTube Football Fantastic!* is packed full of tales which prove those who play and follow the beautiful game really are bonkers.

There's plenty more bizarre funnies, including the unfortunate Sky Sports reporter who fell off a ladder on live TV, the Danish player who was bombarded with dead rats and the strange case of the French star who was sent off before kick-off!

Every story featured in the book comes powered with a link to a YouTube clip of the incident, so you can watch the assorted examples of managerial madness, footballer fails, ridiculous referee blunders and fan mayhem online in all their glory.

This book is a must-read for all those who love the game and know that when you get 22 players out on a pitch – and thousands in the stands – it's only a matter of time before something will go hilariously wrong.

BACK OF THE NET

Goals come in all shapes and sizes – they all count, after all – but there's nothing quite like an eye-catching wonder goal to light up any match.

▶ Wonderful Wazza

http://y2u.be/GpSwJWr-hMI

Beating off some seriously stiff competition from a whole host of other glorious contenders, Wayne Rooney's amazing overhead bicycle kick against Manchester City in February 2011 was voted the greatest goal of the first 20 years of the Premier League. The Manchester United forward had only bagged four league goals in seven months before this one, but his fantastic fifth – arrowed into the top corner from ten yards out – silenced the critics and proved the England star could still do the business.

▼ Incredible Ibrahimovic

http://y2u.be/Ck5P30zC3Z0

Zlatan Ibrahimovic has always been a special player, and he was at his truly spectacular best in 2010 against England. Keeper Joe Hart came out to head the ball away from danger but, unluckily for him, his clearance fell to the big Swede 35 yards out. In a flash, the striker decided to go for goal and opted for an amazing bicycle kick volley that sailed over the stunned England defenders and found the back of the net.

AN AMAZING IBRA HAT-TRICK

▼ Brilliant Brazil

http://y2u.be/M5HbmeNKino

Before Spain and Germany's golden generations came along, Brazil's 1970 side were considered to be the best on the planet, and their final goal in the World Cup final against Italy typified their brilliance. Later described as "the perfect goal", Brazil stylishly worked the ball out of defence past a series of bewildered Italians before Pele casually teed up the rampaging right back Carlos Alberto on the right-hand edge of the penalty area to deliver an unstoppable low shot.

◄ Mario's Rocket

http://y2u.be/Uvuuc0fVZFg

Sometimes the greatest goals come when they're least expected. That was the case when Italy beat Germany in the Euro 2012 semi-final thanks to a belter from Mario Balotelli. There seemed little danger when Riccardo Montolivo hit a hopeful pass forward, but Super Mario was first to react, bursting clear of the German defence and unleashing a sizzling shot from 18 yards that smashed into the roof of the net.

KICK-OFF TIME

Football's meant to be about the 90 minutes of action, but there are times that events before kick-off are as equally as entertaining as the match itself.

◀ Diana's Debacle

http://y2u.be/9EBIDJLI7a4

Celebrities love getting involved in major football events, but legendary singer Diana Ross probably wishes she hadn't bothered after providing one of those hide-behind-the-pillow moments at the 1994 World Cup opening ceremony. All the Motown star had to do was mime her way through a song before kicking a ball into an open net from three yards away. The plan was for the net to break in two on impact, releasing a thousand white balloons in the process, but somehow, embarrassingly, Ross toe-poked her shot wide of the target.

▶ Cry Baby

http://y2u.be/b1kusL894tM

Playing at the World Cup finals can be an emotional experience, but crying your eyes out in front of billions of watching fans around the globe is still a bit over the top. North Korea striker Jong Tae-Se shot to worldwide fame in 2010 when TV cameras captured him blubbering his way through the entire national anthem before their clash with Brazil. The fact that he put his teammates to shame with his teary patriotism was quite surprising, given the fact that he was actually born in Japan to two South Korean parents.

GAZZA HOULD BE PROUD

▲ Evra's Pre-match Meltdown

http://y2u.be/5ZKynfYDZC4

French defender Patrice Evra really livened up the pre-match warm-up ahead of Marseilles' Europa League clash with Guimaraes in 2017 but, unfortunately, it was for all the wrong reasons, as the full-back took exception to something one of his own supporters said to him. Cue Evra launching a flying kick over the advertising hoardings to the head of the talkative fan, which earned him a red card from the referee before the match had even started and a charge of violent conduct from UEFA.

▼ Roman's Ritual

http://y2u.be/VUWLqL1l3sc

Borussia Dortmund goalkeeper Roman Burki is a superstitious soul and has earned himself something of a reputation in Germany thanks to his quirky pre-match ritual. The Swiss stopper just can't resist getting his hands on the match ball before kick-off and, when the referee and captains head to the centre circle for the toss, Burki is always lurking in the background, ready to "pinch" the ball from the officials or the girl or boy acting as the match-day mascot.

HoW DID THEY MISS THAT?

Every player dreams of scoring, but sometimes that dream can turn into a nightmare when the ball just refuses to go into the back of the net.

▶ The Iwelumo Incident

http://y2u.be/59sG34Nx-DY

A very embarrassing example of missing a completely open goal, Scotland striker Chris Iwelumo was left scratching his head in utter disbelief when he failed to score against Norway at Hampden Park back in 2008. Teammate Gary Naysmith must have been pretty confused as well after watching Iwelumo meet his inch-perfect cross just a metre from the goal only to inexplicably side-foot the ball back toward him, rather than past the stranded Norwegian goalkeeper.

▼ Taxi for Torres

http://y2u.be/e2E-5PyYjT0

Fernando Torres cost Chelsea £50 million, but the Blues definitely didn't get value for money from their big-money signing when they faced Manchester United in 2011. To be fair, the Spanish striker did score in the game at Old Trafford, but Torres still hit the headlines for all the wrong reasons when he took the ball past United goalkeeper David de Gea but then stuck out an awkward left foot and stabbed his shot wide of the post with the goal at his mercy.

MUST HAVE BEEN SOMETHING IN THE AIR, FERNANDO

Keep It Simple

http://y2u.be/SVGSd2hk6No

One of the golden rules of finishing is not to over-complicate things. Shame then that Qatar's Fahad Khalfan didn't follow the rule when his side faced Uzbekistan at the Asian Games in 2010. Khalfan got the ball after one of the Uzbekistan defenders sold his keeper short with a back pass but, as he raced toward the now unguarded goal, the striker decided to showboat and hit the ball with the outside of his left boot. His unwise effort kept curling, hit the post and bounced clear.

▲ The Madness of Mario

http://y2u.be/Ea6t_FCQ6Vc

Some misses are the result of nerves, but there are some which can be blamed squarely on the idiocy of the player. This was definitely the case when Mario Balotelli was on the pitch for Manchester City against LA Galaxy in their 2011 pre-season friendly in America. Clean through on goal, the Italian striker thought he'd be clever and pirouetted on the ball before trying to back-heel it past the Galaxy keeper. The effort went wide, while manager Roberto Mancini just went ballistic.

▲ Villa the Villain

http://y2u.be/K8kQRA2sB60

Spain won the World Cup in 2010, but star striker David Villa definitely wasn't on world-beating form a few months later when the champions faced Colombia in a friendly in Madrid, hitting the post with the goal at his mercy and then slamming the rebound so wide that the ball actually went out for a throw-in. Luckily for Villa, he did find the back of the net five minutes from time to avoid a dressing down in the dressing room.

Crisis for Cristiano

http://y2u.be/9YTPxNIf5is

Even the greatest players can have an unexplained horror show in front of goal, as Cristiano Ronaldo proved in 2006 when playing for Manchester United against Sheffield United. Wayne Rooney started the attack near the corner flag. Ryan Giggs got the ball on the edge of the area and delivered a pinpoint pass to Ronaldo, who was all alone in the six-yard box. How the Portuguese then managed to scoop his effort over the bar was a complete mystery.

SIDELINE SILLINESS

These memorable incidents are proof positive that what happens in the team dugout can be just as lively as what happens out on the field of play.

▼ Head Banger

http://y2u.be/ej9qwhfqOGI

The 2011 Mexican Cup semi-final between Morelia and Cruz Azul was a bad-tempered match and descended into violence when an angry Azul fan ran on the pitch to pick a fight with one his own players. In the chaos, Azul keeper Jesus Corona made his way toward the opposition dugout for a "chat" with Morelia assistant manager Sergio Martin. At first, it seemed as if the pair were holding hands and enjoying a friendly conversation, but TV cameras then caught Corona kick Martin in the groin before headbutting his face.

▼ Mind the Gap

http://y2u.be/EOrKYm8hp38

Jose Mourinho is usually a rather cool dude but, when he was Real Madrid manager, he was left distinctly red faced during a Spanish league match against Getafe in 2011. The Portuguese embarrassingly tripped up on the slippery steps leading down to the visitors' dugout and came a complete cropper. The Getafe supporters roared with delight at his misfortune, while Mourinho unsuccessfully tried to style it out by keeping his head down.

Sherwood's Stitch

http://y2u.be/I3X5_uqQNjo

Supporters are never shy when it comes to telling managers what they're doing wrong. It happens at every single game, but Spurs boss Tim Sherwood decided to turn the tables on one particularly talkative Tottenham fan in 2014 by inviting him to sit in his seat in the White Hart Lane dugout. The chap had, apparently, spent all season telling Sherwood from the stands what substitutions to make and the boss finally decided to call his bluff and invite him down to the bench during a game.

THAT'S NOT FOOTBALL!

The beautiful game as we know it has been around for more than 150 years but the history of ball sports goes back even further.

▼ No Murders, Please!

http://y2u.be/Ifh_FxQDafk

The slightly insane residents of Atherstone in Warwickshire have been playing their traditional "Shrove Tuesday Ball Game" for centuries, and there's only one rule – players cannot kill each other. There are no teams and no goals and the aim is to be the one holding the heavy leather ball at the end of all the madness. The game celebrated its 800th anniversary in 1999 and usually kicks offs at 3.00 p.m. and lasts for a couple of hours, although the bruised villagers are usually nursing their injuries for weeks after the final whistle.

Sport of Emperors

http://y2u.be/kOXvTk-PVxc

Legend has it that a Chinese emperor by the name of Huangdi came up with the game called "Cuju" around 4,500 years ago as a way of preparing his soldiers for battle, but it remains something of a mystery how a sport in which the players kicked a ball to each other actually helped to win any wars. Unlike modern football, the aim of Cuju was not to score goals, but to score the most points, with points deducted from the 12 to 16 players on each side for both short and over-hit passes, as well as for kicking the ball out of play.

LET'S HOPE THIS RULE WASN'T MADE TO BE BROKEN...

▶ Calcio Kicks

http://y2u.be/ksJtH2CCCUY

Created in the Italian city of Florence over 500 years ago, "Calcio Fiorentino" (Florentine kick game) is still played today and, if you've got a huge sandpit, 54 players (27 per team), 8 referees and 50 minutes spare, you could have a match. Players can use their feet and hands, and goals are scored by throwing the ball over a spot on the perimeter of the square pitch. Headbutting, choking and punching are all legal, but they do draw the line at kicks to the head.

▼ Aerial Bombardment

http://y2u.be/1MGp_sQHQLc

Basically an early Japanese version of keepie-up, "Kemari" is nearly 1,500 years old and involves a team of players repeatedly heading, kicking and even elbowing a small sphere in a desperate attempt to stop it hitting the ground. The ball – called the "Mari" – was traditionally made from deerskin and was probably the inspiration for the modern hacky sack. Former US President George W. Bush even had a crack at the sport when he visited Japan back in 1992.

THE ANCIENT ART OF KEEPIE-UPPIE

Eton Antics

http://y2u.be/p78rHOIQ2iA

The complete laws of the famous "Eton Field Game" would give a rocket scientist a headache but, to try and cut a very long story short, it's a 200-year-old sport devised by Eton School that mixes a bit of football and rugby. Teams can score a goal for three points by hitting the back of the opposition net, but there are five points on offer if they can score a "rogue" by booting the ball off an opposition player and deflecting it over their goal line at one end of the pitch. A player then has to touch the ball to complete the "rogue" and avoid getting a detention from the PE teacher.

CHAOS IN THE STUDIO

Television brings the beautiful game to millions of fans but sometimes football broadcasts don't quite go according to plan.

▶ Alarming Interruption

http://y2u.be/i68fVnbWefY

Carrying on regardless is a very British trait and was the order of the day in 2016 at the BBC as its live Saturday-afternoon show, "Football Focus" went out. Host Dan Walker and pundits Martin Keown and Mark Lawrenson were happily chatting away about the day's upcoming fixtures when the fire alarm went off, followed by a recorded message telling staff to evacuate the building, but the brave trio completely ignored the potential inferno and carried on with the programme.

DON'T TRY THIS AT HOME

▶ Light Down!

http://y2u.be/KmFya5wYy7I

The joys of keepie-uppie are probably best enjoyed outdoors where there's plenty of room. Juggling indoors is just asking for trouble, as this clip of a chap with a football in a TV studio disastrously proves. He's clearly got some skills, but it all goes spectacularly wrong when he decides to give the ball a bit of welly and manages to smash it into one of the studio's ceiling lights, bringing it down to the floor with a massive crash.

▲ Studio Strop

http://y2u.be/6Sviu9I3bew

Louis van Gaal is one of the Netherlands' most successful managers, but the former Man United boss completely lost the plot on Dutch TV in 2009. All was well until the host of the Champions League show revealed live on air that two new pundits, and not van Gaal, would be joining him on next week's programme. The ex-Holland manager didn't like what he heard and launched into a rant in front of the cameras before removing his microphone and marching out of the studio.

TV Tantrum

http://y2u.be/2vtlErna5Rk

Football presenters are supposed to the professionals but sometimes even the best pundits can get over-excited in the heat of the moment. Step forward the four Norwegians who were covering their national team's game with San Marino in Oslo in 2016 and were so upset when the opposition scored that they totally lost their cool in the studio, shouting and banging the desk in disbelief. Their childish outburst was only cut short when the studio lights suddenly went off, and they had time to think about their petulant behaviour.

▶ Kamara's Calamity

http://y2u.be/McdjBaChdBA

Sky Sports' "Soccer Saturday" is an unmissable show for many football fans at the weekend and, back in 2010, they were treated to one of the funniest moments in the history of live TV when host Jeff Stelling spoke to reporter Chris Kamara at the Portsmouth-versus-Blackburn game. "We're off to Fratton Park," Stelling said, "where there's been a red card, but for who, Chris Kamara?" The confused look on Kamara's face said it all. "I don't know, Jeff. Has there?" he replied. "I must have missed that." Cue fits of laughter in the studio as Kamara desperately tried to work out what the hell was going on.

"UNBELIEVABLE!"

SUPER STRIKES

Football's all about goals and, as these brilliant scores prove, sometimes it needs a moment of pure genius to find the back of the net.

▼ Magical Maradona

http://y2u.be/1wVho3l0NtU

The 1986 World Cup quarterfinal between Argentina and England may be infamous for Maradona's "Hand of God" goal, but he did also score a sensational (and perfectly legal) second goal. Starting with a pirouette and burst of acceleration in his own half, the Argentinean maestro slalomed majestically through the statuesque England team before rounding Peter Shilton in goal. Named "Goal of the Century" in 2000, it remains a mystery how so many disgruntled England supporters voted for the Argentinean's effort after his earlier skulduggery.

SKILL OR SORCERY?

▶ Quick Thinking

http://y2u.be/Qe7k1sH0BkA

The second half of Everton's Europa League clash with Hadjuk Split in 2017 was only 13 seconds old when Gylfi Sigurdsson scored this unbelievable screamer. The Icelander stole the ball from an opponent near the halfway line but, rather than opt for the simple pass, he spotted the Split goalkeeper off his line and decided to try his luck with an audacious 50-yard effort. His radar was spot on, and the ball sailed gloriously over the stopper and into the goal.

Daring David

http://y2u.be/tOSpLQNNdcs

Another example of a classic long-range strike, David Villa's goal for New York City against Philadelphia Union in the MLS in 2017 was a real beauty. New York broke out of defence but there seemed no real danger, even when Villa stole the ball from the defender on the halfway line. The Spain star had other ideas and hit a hopeful shot into the sky. The Philadelphia keeper desperately back-peddled as the ball dropped out of the heavens, but it was too late and Villa had scored a cracker.

▼ Classy Cristiano

http://y2u.be/oqiKmC0qhZw

There's no better time to produce a wonder goal than in Spain's "El Clásico" between Real Madrid and Barcelona, which is exactly what Cristiano Ronaldo did at the Nou Camp in 2017. Madrid broke from deep in their own half and, before Braca could recover, Ronaldo was racing down the left with the ball at his feet. Three defenders managed to get back, but the Portuguese didn't care as he smashed a sublime, curling shot from the edge of the area that rocketed into the top corner.

A CLASICO CLINCHER

OFFSIDE ODDITIES

The offside law is one of football's trickiest rules to understand and even the best players and referees can get rather confused.

A SLICK PIECE OF BUSINESS

◀ Sheikh on It

http://y2u.be/wmjoN3_Hhtl

"Playing to the whistle" is one of football's most famous clichés, but the Kuwait national team took the old saying a little too literally during their 1982 World Cup clash with France when the entire team heard a shrill blast and immediately stopped, assuming the referee had blown for offside. The problem was the referee hadn't actually made a sound and, taking full advantage of Kuwait's sudden halt, France scored. Chaos ensued as the Kuwaiti officials stormed the pitch in protest and, after he was promised a few hundred barrels of oil, the referee finally disallowed the goal.

Soviet Sickener

http://y2u.be/hXk4-xSRl6g

Diego Maradona's "Hand of God" made the headlines during the 1986 World Cup, but the tournament was not without more controversy, and those who witnessed the USSR's last-16 clash with Belgium are probably still scratching their heads after the clueless linesman failed to spot that Jan Cuelemans was at least five yards offside when he scored a crucial late equalizer for the Belgians. The outrageous "goal" took the match into extra-time and, to add insult to injury, the Belgians went on to clinch a 4-3 victory.

▼ Messi's Misjudgement

http://y2u.be/Kuo53eEAySc

Nobody does spectacular goals quite like Lionel Messi and the Argentine magician conjured up another cracker for Barcelona against Eibar in 2017, brilliantly nutmegging the helpless opposition goalkeeper with a first-time side-foot chop. The Spanish bookmakers immediately stopped taking bets on "Goal of the Season", but Messi's joy quickly turned to disappointment when replays revealed he was two metres offside and his wonder strike was chalked off by the referee.

NOT THIS TIME, LEO

▶ Inept Linesman

http://y2u.be/eCgkZCacw8Q

As all students of football know, you can't be offside from a throw-in. No one knows exactly why, but that's one of the laws of the game and, if you're going to pursue a career as a professional linesman, you really should be up to speed on the rules. The assistant referee running the line in Melbourne Hearts's game with Brisbane Roar in 2013 sadly wasn't and made a complete fool of himself when he raised his flag for offside directly from a Melbourne throw-in. The bemused look on the Melbourne players' faces was priceless.

PITCH INVADERS

A football field is supposed to be only for the players and match officials, and these strange tales show why everyone else really should keep off the grass.

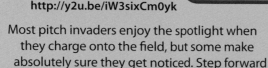

◀ Comical Superhero

http://y2u.be/iW3sixCm0yk

Most pitch invaders enjoy the spotlight when they charge onto the field, but some make absolutely sure they get noticed. Step forward Sunderland fan Bradley Minto, who raced on the grass at the Stadium of Light during his side's game with Man City in 2014 in a full-length Spiderman costume. The crowd thought it hilarious, but the police did not and arrested and charged the trespassing teenager. Luckily for him, he avoided jail but had to pay a £100 fine.

MORE BRUCE LEE THAN PETER SCHMEICHEL

Chase Me!

http://y2u.be/U0Z_dowc3dQ

The thrill for many pitch invaders is evading capture by the stewards or police, prolonging their 15 minutes of fame on the pitch for as long as possible. The supporter who gatecrashed Russia's World Cup qualifier with Luxembourg definitely wanted to stay out there and easily evaded three clumsy stewards before outsprinting a policeman. In the end, he was only caught after diving head first into one of the goals, allowing the copper to finally get his hands on him.

▼ Kung Fu Keeper

http://y2u.be/JmOSGlRV4-Y

Eager stewards and fleet-footed policemen are the natural enemies of the pitch invader, but the Dutch Cup clash between Ajax and AZ Alkmaar in 2011 proved that angry goalkeepers can be equally dangerous. The keeper in question was Alkmaar's Esteban Alvarado, who took violent exception to a foray onto the pitch by a 19-year-old Ajax fan, flooring him spectacularly with a kung fu kick. Alvarado put the boot in twice more as the teenager lay prone – just seconds before the referee showed him the red card.

Wheels in Motion

http://y2u.be/SOZWFbT_E_0

Last-gasp goals can make even the most level-headed supporter go a bit crazy, which is exactly what happened when Northampton Town equalized against Rotherham United at the Sixfields Stadium in 2011. Cue teenager Derry Felton, who drove his motorized wheelchair across the pitch in celebration and, in the process, became an instant Internet hit. "I didn't know what was happening and then I was in the middle of the pitch and I just thought, how did I get here?" Felton admitted. "It was just a spur-of-the-moment thing and I never thought it would end up on YouTube."

▲ Power Prank

http://y2u.be/dfg-5l_z7yc

The pre-match team photo is an old tradition and, back in 2001, it presented Mancunian prankster Karl Power with the ideal opportunity to pull off one the most audacious pranks in football history when Manchester United faced Bayern Munich in the Champions League. Power got past security by pretending to be part of a TV crew and, once pitch side at Old Trafford, he changed into his kit and casually strolled out with the rest of the United players for a cheeky photo.

CHART HOPEFULS

All top footballers have incredible natural talent but, sadly, they sometimes mistakenly think it's for music, rather than for kicking a ball about.

▲ Savage Slaven

http://y2u.be/-RYg8Dy3xk4

Croatia's Slaven Bilic was known as a tough and temperamental defender in his playing days with West Ham, Everton and Hajduk Split, so it came as no surprise when he joined a band called Rawbau, which recorded a song called "Atreno Ludil" (Fiery Madness). Bilic played rhythm guitar on the single, which the rockers released to coincide with the 2008 European Championships, and the patriotic Croatian public thought it was anything but crazy, as the song went straight to Number One.

▼ Wheels of Steel

http://y2u.be/NSuhRGCWbgM

Many footballers have tried their luck as DJs, but flamboyant French striker Djibril Cisse reckoned he was so good on the "wheels of steel" that he decided to release his own CD mix of his favourite dance tunes in 2008. Entitled *Music and Me: The DJ Inside Me*, the album featured a track called "Got To Get Away", which probably struck a chord with fans of any of the 12 different clubs he's played for.

◀ Cruyff's Cringe

http://y2u.be/AfX9uwL0F2k

Dutch legend Johan Cruyff is famous for the legendary "turn" he invented, and which is named after him. He's not famous, however, for his singing career, which began (and, thankfully, ended) in 1969 and, after listening to his single – "Oei Oei Oei (Dat Was Me Weer een Loei)" – you'll know exactly why. The oom-pah-style song is truly terrible and, if you listen very, very carefully, you can almost hear Cruyff dying of embarrassment as the band plays on.

BEWARE THE BACK PASS

It might seem simple, but playing the ball back to the goalkeeper can be one of the most dangerous decisions a player can make in a match.

▶ Disaster for Dixon

http://y2u.be/GUwVPNFaUK8

Lee Dixon enjoyed a glittering career with Arsenal and England, but the Gunners defender also dropped a few clangers during his 20 years as a player. His most embarrassing mistake came in 1991 when Arsenal faced Coventry at Highbury. The full-back received the ball 40 yards out from his own goal and with no options ahead of him, decided to knock it back to goalkeeper David Seaman. Unfortunately, Dixon didn't bother to check where Seaman actually was and skilfully chipped his bemused teammate with a curling but calamitous back pass.

A Very Early Bath

http://y2u.be/Vt61k9P1PEA

A badly placed back pass at any time during a match is ill-advised but straight from the kick-off is simply suicidal, as Ebbsfleet United's Ryan Blake found out in 2011 during a league game against Farnborough when his limp early effort was intercepted by Kezie Ibe. The Farnborough striker raced toward goal, only to be brought down in the area by goalkeeper Preston Edwards, who was promptly shown a red card by the referee after just 10 seconds.

Achilles Heel

http://y2u.be/p8EpsBbizXI

Spanish footballers are famous for their silky skills, but they deserted defender Inigo Martinez while on Under-21 duty for his country in 2011 against Georgia. There seemed little danger when the Georgian keeper launched a hopeful long-range punt up the field, but Martinez couldn't resist making an unconventional back pass, volleying the ball with an eye-catching back heel. Unfortunately, his effort ballooned off his boot, over his irate keeper and into the net from a full 40 yards out.

WE BLAME THE GROUNDSMAN

▲ Three Lions Lose

http://y2u.be/05ds1Q5vFEY

England had lead France 1-0 in their Euro 2004 group-stage game in Lisbon but ended up losing 2-1 thanks to a moment of injury-time madness from midfielder Steven Gerrard. The Liverpool star didn't see Thierry Henry lurking and hit a sloppy back pass, which the France striker gratefully intercepted. David James brought Henry down in the area as he tried to round the goalkeeper, and Zinedine Zidane stepped forward to score from the penalty spot and seal a dramatic victory for Les Bleus.

◄ The Danger of Divets

http://y2u.be/abioqGXPQdU

Bumpy pitches are always nightmare for players at all levels of the beautiful game and even top-class internationals should be wary of the dangers of an uneven surface. Just ask England goalkeeper Paul Robinson, who had to reluctantly pick the ball out of his own net in a Euro 2008 qualifier against Croatia in Zagreb after Gary Neville's back pass hit a divet and bobbled badly, meaning the keeper's swinging right boot hit thin air, rather than the ball.

WE ARE THE CHAMPIONS!

Winning a trophy is the perfect end to the season but the excitement of getting their hands on silverware sometimes causes footballers to rather lose the plot.

Keeper Calamity

http://y2u.be/zsCELZPsI5g

Netherlands goalkeeper Maarten Stekelenburg had a superb 2010–11 season, as Ajax were crowned Dutch champions, but his normally safe hands spectacularly deserted him on an open-top bus ride through Amsterdam, when he dropped the trophy as he tried to pass it to teammate Jan Vertonghen. Fortunately, an eagle-eyed policeman picked up the silverware before it was squashed by traffic and handed it to an eager Ajax supporter, who raced after the bus on foot in a desperate but hilarious effort to return the trophy.

▼ On My Head, Son

http://y2u.be/CgyJR-1LYvE

Kicks to the head are an occupational hazard in football, but players don't usually expect to get a size nine to the face after the final whistle has been blown. It happened, however, to Antonio Cassano in 2012 in the aftermath of AC Milan's goalless draw with Roma – a result which gave the club the Italian title – when he was giving a post-match interview

but was violently interrupted by team-mate Zlatan Ibrahimovic karate kicking the side of his head. Hopefully, the pair kissed and made up as the party in the dressing room got into full swing.

◀ Smooth Moves

http://y2u.be/MlGgydMOId4

Plenty of players enjoy an impromptu dance on the pitch after winning a trophy, but midfielder Kevin-Prince Boateng took things to a whole new level in 2011 after AC Milan were crowned Serie A champions, dressing up in a Michael Jackson costume for the occasion and moonwalking inside the San Siro to the song "Billie Jean". Boateng was cheered along by his Milan teammates, while his agent immediately began negotiations with the Italian version of "Strictly Come Dancing".

▲ Butter Fingers

http://y2u.be/yYNyc_myTz0

With the exception of goalkeepers, footballers aren't really known for their handling skills, and Real Madrid's Sergio Ramos proved that players are definitely better with their feet when he dropped the Copa del Rey trophy in 2011. Madrid were parading the cup on an open-top bus through the city after beating arch rivals Barcelona in the final when Ramos lifted it onto his head but, disastrously, let it slip through his fingers, sending the silverware crashing onto the road and underneath the wheels of the bus following behind.

▶ Morrow's Agony

http://y2u.be/XYNf1cf8ZMw

Ending up in hospital just hours after scoring the winner in a major cup final is far from the ideal way to celebrate victory, but it happened to Steve Morrow in 1993 after Arsenal beat Sheffield Wednesday in the League Cup. Morrow found the back of the net in the 68th minute but was denied the chance to party when teammate Tony Adams picked him up after the final whistle – and then dropped him. The Northern Ireland midfielder broke his arm as he fell and was whisked off to get a cast on the injury in the local A&E.

"THANKS A LOT TONY!"

OFF THE BALL!

Proof that football can be a comedy goldmine, even when the ball itself is nowhere to be seen.

▼ Mayor Mayhem

http://y2u.be/YO9F6BDffx4

Charity matches are meant to be friendly affairs, but former Mayor of London Boris Johnson spectacularly ignored such niceties during an England-versus-Germany Legends game in 2006. Much to the amusement of the 15,000 fans inside Reading's Madejski Stadium, mop-haired Boris charged like a rampant bull toward one of the German players but, unfortunately, began to lose his balance and ended up crashing head first into his opponent's groin, flattening him in the process.

Bottoms Up

http://y2u.be/dX_o3IrZkeg

Spanish hardmen didn't come any tougher or more volatile than Sevilla centre half Pablo Alfaro, a player who was willing to do almost anything to win all three points for his team. Aside from being remembered for a whole host of truly terrible tackles, the dirty defender is perhaps best known for shoving his hand up the bottom of a rather shocked Atletico Madrid front man during a 2004 Copa del Rey clash. Now, that's what you call man-to-man marking.

◀ Hollywood Hooligan

http://y2u.be/vGJ3nHS1RXU

Before becoming a movie star, Vinnie Jones spent most of his time in the Wimbledon midfield scaring the hell out of anyone stupid enough to come anywhere near him and, back in February 1988 during a match at home to Newcastle United, Paul Gascoigne made the foolhardy decision to wander over and mark vicious Vinnie at a free kick. In an instant, the would-be actor stepped back onto Gazza's toes, reached behind him and promptly grabbed the terrified teenager's testicles.

Timely Trip

http://y2u.be/4T7Jz0XoLrc

Not all off-the-ball incidents are worthy of a place in the game's Hall of Shame, as Adrian Jesus Bastia proved during a Greek Super League clash between Panathinaikos and Asteras Tripolis in 2008. Enraged by Panathinaikos' poor performance, one rebellious fan ran onto the pitch in protest and was chased by a less-than-athletic bunch of local riot police. Doing his good deed for the day, Argentine Bastia cleverly tripped the invader so that he could finally be apprehended but was harshly rewarded for his quick thinking with a red card by the referee and an early bath.

THE ULTIMATE FOOTBALL HARD MAN

Short Shrift

http://y2u.be/E8RHBeBsTek

The 2011 Greek league clash between Olympiakos and AEK Athens was a typically fierce affair, but there was also a sublime moment of comedy when Olympiakos defender Francois Modesto decided to take revenge for a crunching challenge from AEK player Cala, pulling his shorts down to his ankles to reveal a rather fetching pair of white Y-fronts. An ironic case of Modesto ensuring Cala was not allowed to keep his modesty.

AMAZING SAVES

It's tough being a goalkeeper but all their mistakes and misjudgments are forgiven when they pull off incredible goal-saving stops.

▲ Hugo the Hero

http://y2u.be/LG2lDe9NT_Q

French stopper Hugo Lloris must have felt very lonely during Spurs' Champions League clash with Real Madrid in 2017. The Spanish giants were on the attack and, when they swung in a cross, the Tottenham defence all went completely AWOL. It seemed certain the unmarked Karim Benzema would score with his head from only two yards out until Lloris spread himself bravely in front of the striker and somehow managed to keep the effort out with his legs.

Rapid Recovery

http://y2u.be/KSRB630S3ak

All goalkeepers make mistakes and Peru Under-21 Angelo Campos definitely dropped a clanger against Uruguay in 2013 when he raced out to clear a through ball. He missed and the Uruguay striker shot from outside the area but Campos refused to give up, sprinting back just in time to dramatically stop the ball on the line. The danger wasn't over, however, as the forward followed up but Campos was up and completed a miraculous double save with his outstretched legs on the goal line.

The Scorpion

http://y2u.be/wkYmmV7Oa-U

When a goalkeeper earns the nickname "The Madman", it's safe to assume he'll be entertaining, and custodian Rene Higuita certainly lived up to his billing in 1995 when Colombia played England at Wembley with an unbelievable "scorpion kick" save. England midfielder Jamie Redknapp punted a harmless-looking shot toward the goal from long range but, rather than taking the safe option of actually catching the ball, Higuita leaped dramatically forward and cleared the danger in mid-air with the heels of both boots.

▲ Safe Hands

SEAMAN'S HEROICS

http://y2u.be/VTBkWRs7r-c

Arsenal were the red-hot favourites to beat Sheffield United in their 2003 FA Cup semi-final showdown, but the Gunners had an incredible save from keeper David Seaman – aka "Safe Hands" – to thank for their victory. Blades striker Paul Peschisolido was the man who thought he had scored with a header from close range, only for Seaman to contort his body backwards and claw the effort out with his right hand just a second before it would have crossed the line.

▶ Top-corner Miracle

http://y2u.be/a6HdqF5dQ7Y

Natural athleticism is a key skill for a top-class keeper and Manchester United's David de Gea proved he had it in buckets in a 2016 Premier League clash with Liverpool at Anfield. An attack from the home side saw midfielder Philippe Coutinho on the ball 35 yards from goal and the Brazilian produced a stunning, curling shot that was heading for the top corner. Cue a sensational reflex leap from the Spanish keeper, flying high and wide to palm the ball over the crossbar.

THE MEN IN BLACK

A good referee is one you don't notice during a game but, unfortunately, these officials were anything but anonymous.

Sozzled Shmolik

http://y2u.be/IO_ncT_fsKc

The pressures of refereeing are enough to make any stressed official indulge in a post-match drink, but Belarusian whistler Sergei Shmolik turned to the bottle before kick-off in 2008 with disastrous results. Refereeing a league clash between Vitebsk and Naftan, Shmolik was so tipsy that he spent most of the match staggering around the centre circle, refusing to issue a single card despite some tasty tackles and, when post-match tests revealed he was seriously over the limit, the Belarusian FA promptly suspended him.

▶ Triple Jeopardy

http://y2u.be/d-NRQz0P6vg

Everyone knows that two yellow cards equal an early bath. Everyone except English referee Graham Poll that is, who disastrously decided to rip up the rule book during the 2006 World Cup in Germany when he showed Croatia's Josip Simunic three yellows before finally giving him his marching orders against Australia. Only Poll knows why he didn't send Simunic off after his second booking, but the penny did finally drop when the Croatian committed yet another foul and the forgettable Englishman scribbled his name down in the book for a third time.

Armed and Dangerous

http://y2u.be/8_7yYFbsL_M

Everybody has their breaking point and Brazilian referee Gabriel Murta obviously reached his during an amateur game between Brumadinho and Amantes da Bola in 2015. Poor old Murta was kicked and punched by an Amantes player and, rather than reach for his book, the irate official (who's day job was with the police) headed to his dressing room and remerged clutching a handgun. Thankfully, one of Murta's linesman persuaded him not to use it, so no one was shot.

▲ Dangerous Dane

http://y2u.be/RLXPGE7VWDw

Awarding a penalty is always a controversial moment and, as Herbert Fandel learned in 2007, it can also prove potentially painful for the referee in question. Fandel was officiating a Euro 2008 qualifier between Denmark and Sweden in Copenhagen when he gave the visitors a late spot kick, prompting outraged Danish fan Ronni Norvig to invade the pitch and try to punch him. Luckily for the ref, a Danish player stepped in to save him and the game was abandoned. Sweden were awarded a 3-0 win, Norvig was fined £210,000 and Fandel sensibly decided never to award a penalty again.

▼ The Probert Sandwich

http://y2u.be/AIB-vRpymKA

A top referee should always be in the right place at the right time, but sometimes their positional sense can let them down. Just ask Lee Probert, who got a painful reminder of the importance of keeping out of the players' way during Fulham's league fixture with Wigan. The official was happily minding his own business as the ball went loose and didn't have enough time to react as two players slid in to regain possession, sandwiching the hapless Probert in a meaty – if accidental – double tackle. The noise of his subsequent whistle was, of course, drowned out by the laughter of the crowd.

BUT WHO GETS THE FREE KICK?

LET'S DANCE!

Football's an exciting game and it should come as no surprise when fans get carried away and simply have to throw some shapes.

Airline Antics

http://y2u.be/jAF2hZxdFRE

Benfica fans were confused when a group of air stewardesses strolled out on the pitch before kick-off at the Estádio da Luz in 2015. What the Emirates airline staff were doing at the game was initially a mystery but all became clearer when they launched into a spoof safety announcement routine, which had the Portuguese crowd in stitches. For example, in the event of a Benfica goal, the PA system announced, supporters were told to place their scarves over their heads and breathe normally.

▲ Dutch Delight

http://y2u.be/UVRXiSxHcR8

The Dutch national team has a reputation for stylish total football, but their supporters in Germany for the 2006 World Cup finals were not quite as easy on the eye, judging by their enthusiastic but chaotic conga on the streets of Frankfurt. The sea of orange they created with their thousands of replica shirts was certainly something to behold but, after perhaps one too many liquid refreshments, it all got a bit silly by the end.

◀ Party People

http://y2u.be/JcbX3OmcBP8

Brazil is famous for its samba and, pretty much anywhere and everywhere fans of the country's team travel, you'll see them dancing in the streets as well as in the stadium. This particular example comes from the 2006 World Cup finals in Germany and proved, yet again, that the South American supporters really don't need much of an excuse for an impromptu party wherever they go.

IS ANYONE WATCHING THE GAME?

▲ Manchester Mayhem

http://y2u.be/nHo07AI_J_k

They say imitation is the sincerest form of flattery, and Manchester City supporters were seriously impressed when Polish side Lech Poznan visited Eastlands for a Europa League game in 2010. However, it wasn't the visitors' beautiful football that caught the City faithful's eye, but rather their unique dance moves as the Poles repeatedly turned their back on the action, put their arms around each other and bounced up and down. The City fans immediately decided to "borrow" the routine and their trademark "Poznan" dance was born.

▶ Street Skills

http://y2u.be/4JXxpZOWtNY

A new dance craze, "Street Style" is a cool mash-up between breakdancing and juggling a football, in which two players go head-to-head in front of a panel of eagle-eyed judges. Each competitor has 20 seconds to impress with a mix of slick moves, skills and originality before passing the ball on to their rival. It's basically keepie-uppie on the dance floor and is now so popular that there's even a World Series.

THE RED MIST

Players are sometimes sent off when it's not their fault, but sometimes they really only have themselves to blame for their dismissal.

▼ Naughty Neymar

http://y2u.be/nPF9erXTbu4

Modern footballers can be a little vain at times and Brazilian superstar Neymar was no exception in 2011 after scoring for his club, Santos. The playmaker had already been booked before he found the back of the net and ran off to celebrate, producing a mask of his own face and popping it on. The Santos supporters and his team-mates thought it was a scream but the ref thought Neymar had got too big for his boots and showed him the dreaded second yellow card.

Violan the Vandal

http://y2u.be/XJAg_TNTArI

Using your head is good advice if you want to be a footballer, but it was taken a little too literally by Italian Jacopo Violan in 2014 when he scored in a lower-league match. The striker was clearly chuffed with his effort but, rather than celebrate with his teammates, he charged toward the touchline and headbutted the plastic sheeting on the side of the dugout. He fell through it and, although he wasn't hurt, the referee decided his act of vandalism was worth a red card.

▲ Silly Salih

http://y2u.be/b7OnHWblXmQ

Referees aren't really known for their brilliant sense of humour, and official Deniz Bitzel definitely didn't get the joke when he took off Salih Dursen in the Turkish Super Lig clash between Galatasaray and Trabzonspor in 2016. Bitzel had just sent off a Trabzonspor player and, in the scuffle that followed, he dropped his red card. It was picked up by Trabzonspor's Salih Dursun, who brandished it at the referee in a show of defiance. Bitzel, of course, wasn't laughing, grabbing back his card and immediately ordering Dursun off.

GUESS WHO HAD THE LAST LAUGH

▶ Foot Fail

http://y2u.be/TaXH3aFKtts

Match officials tend to stick together and this was very much the case in 2011 when Israeli side Maccabi Tel-Aviv played Stoke City in the Europa League and Maccabi player Yoav Ziv had a little meltdown. Ziv lost a boot in a tasty tackle near the touchline but didn't get the foul he thought he deserved and kicked his footwear straight at the linesman. The referee wasn't going to have his mate treated like that and, despite his desperate attempts to apologize, Ziv was off.

41

▼ Movie Misjudgement

http://y2u.be/xvqN5a6qwtE

It's fair to say David Beckham quite likes the limelight and, if the former England captain isn't posing in his pants or going to the hairdressers again, he's now appearing in films. His cameo in 2017 flop *King Arthur: Legend of the Sword*, however, was perhaps a step even for Goldenballs, as fans stayed away from cinemas in their droves and his performance was savaged by critics. It was a "misguided, fist-biter of a performance" wrote *Empire* magazine's underwhelmed reviewer of Becks' brief appearance on screen.

NO OSCARS
FOR BECKS

THE SHOWBOATS

Some players just can't resist showing off. When it comes off, it looks amazing, but their madcap antics aren't always the best idea.

Juggling Joker

http://y2u.be/Bh19QeyupeQ

Most of us have probably wondered what would happen if we started to juggle the ball in the middle of a game, but Corinthians star Edilson actually tried it during a 1999 Cup final against arch rivals Palmeiras in Brazil. After a brief bout of keepie-up on the halfway line, the striker rolled the ball down the back of his neck but was then booted unceremoniously into the air by several angry Palmeiras players, sparking a 22-man brawl. The match was abandoned, and Edilson was dropped by Brazil for causing the riot.

▼ Gazza's Yellow Gaffe

http://y2u.be/7iYeifVvAV0

When butter-fingered referee Dougie Smith dropped his notebook during a Scottish Premier League clash between Rangers and Hibs in 1995, Paul Gascoigne was the first to notice that the careless official had left his yellow card on the Ibrox turf. The midfield prankster promptly brandished the card in Smith's direction much to the amusement of the fans, but the grumpy referee failed to see the joke, grabbed his card back and booked Gascoigne for his impudence.

Bum Note

http://y2u.be/L9P8otes3_k

Players ripping off their shirts after scoring is a common sight in football, but Arsenal's Sammy Nelson decided to go with an altogether cheekier celebration after finding the back of the net against Coventry in 1979. Charging toward the Gunners fans in the North Bank of Highbury after his goal, Nelson lowered his shorts and exposed his bum. The supporters found it hilarious, but Nelson wasn't laughing when Arsenal fined him two weeks' wages for his ill-advised moon.

◀ Face Change

http://y2u.be/8rqMxnlw39w

Different players react to hostile crowds in different ways and, in 1985, famously mental Liverpool goalkeeper Bruce Grobbelaar decided to have a laugh with the Manchester United fans who had been throwing coins onto the pitch during the game. Rather than chuck the coppers back at the supporters, Grobbelaar picked up a couple of coins, put one over each eye and pulled a series of funny faces, which had the Liverpool fans in stitches but had the exact opposite effect on the Red Devils faithful.

GROBBELAAR PLAYING A BLINDER

Seal of Disapproval

http://y2u.be/JAo0BoCsCTo

Showboating can sometimes be a painful business, as Brazilian midfielder Kerlon discovered when he decided to try out his "seal dribble" in a game for Cruzeiro against Atletico Madrid in 2007. Kerlon flicked the ball up and ran past the opposition as he repeatedly bounced it on his forehead. Unfortunately, Atletico's Diego Rocha was not amused and brought Kerlon's antics to an abrupt end with a hefty forearm smash. Rocha got a red card and a 120-day ban for the attack, while Kerlon got a very sore jaw.

RUNNING THE LINE

The life of the linesmen can be an unforgiving one, as thousands of fans often disagree with your decisions, but, as these clips prove, it can also be very funny indeed.

▼ Stand Up, Man!

http://y2u.be/MozehnOPWjk

Plenty of linesmen have suffered painful blows from the ball in the line of duty, but the man with the flag for the MLS All Stars game with Man United in 2011 was not one of them. The assistant referee was hit in the chest by the ball, but it was the softest contact you could imagine. Nonetheless, he reacted as though he'd been shot by a tank at close range, throwing his arms theatrically in the air before hitting the deck. The embarrassed smile on his face when he got up said it all.

DOWN BUT NOT OUT

Alba Assault

http://y2u.be/KrfXUOfMinQ

Barcelona's Copa del Rey showdown with Atletico Madrid in 2015 wasn't the most exciting game, but the crowd were, at least, kept entertained when the linesman accidentally assaulted one of the Barca players. Raising his flag to signal a throw-in, the linesman had absolutely no idea that Jordi Alba was behind him on the touchline and, as the defender scampered back onto the pitch, the official started to lower his flag and poleaxed the Spanish international.

▲ Sick Day

http://y2u.be/nFaiunaO-zQ

Dundee's SPL game with Kilmarnock took a bizarre and stomach-churning turn in 2017 as the game came to a temporary halt when one of the linesmen suddenly started feeling ill. The poorly official had to briefly abandon his duties to be sick near the corner flag but, if he was hoping for any sympathy from the referee, he was disappointed, as Craig Thompson reached into his pocket and showed his ailing colleague a red card.

Touchline Tumble

http://y2u.be/TrZsuNwKpAU

Sprinting down the line with an eagle eye on the offside line is a tough job and it's perfectly understandable that linesmen sometimes lose sight of everything else. Step forward the assistant referee for Burnley's match against Bristol City in 2013, who was so focused on the action that he failed to spot an injured Bristol player on the touchline and took a spectacular tumble over the footballer. Luckily, it was his pride, rather than anything more serious, that suffered the damage.

▼ Italian Fail

http://y2u.be/TY44vW9q-kk

Football's a fast game, and it proved a little too rapid for the poor linesman at Empoli's Serie A clash with Inter Milan in 2015. The hapless official was caught out by a sudden change of direction in play and, as he desperately tried to readjust and get back into position, he lost his balance and hit the grass. Like a true professional, however, he still managed to flag for offside while sat on the turf.

THEY DIDN'T MEAN THAT!

These inadvertent efforts prove that it really doesn't matter how you score, as long as you get the ball on target.

▶ Back to Goal

http://y2u.be/riaHVWVzFVI

Anything can happen in a goal-mouth scramble, and it did in 2015 when Japanese clubs Zweigen Kanazawa and Kamatamare Sanuki played each other. A spot of penalty-area ping pong in the Sanuki box saw the ball bouncing all over the place, but they seemed to have cleared the danger, only for one of their players to blast it against Kanazawa's Cha Young-Hwan. He had his back turned when the ball made contact, but that didn't stop it spinning off him and into the back of the net.

▶ Wembley Luck

http://y2u.be/HJXcTkbXXMc

Every player dreams of marking their debut for a new club with a goal, and that's just what Mexican Javier Hernandez did for Man United in the Community Shield against Chelsea in 2010. The striker burst into the box at Wembley to get on the end of a cross but his right-footed shot wasn't convincing, and all he managed to do was blast the ball into his own face. Luckily for the new boy, the ball bounced off him and into the net.

▲ Diame's Ankle

http://y2u.be/XTBTUFXNaT4

Corners often cause chaos in the penalty area, and that was certainly the case in 2017 in the match between Newcastle United and Brighton. The Magpies pumped the ball into the box from the corner, but it was partially cleared by the keeper and fell to a Newcastle player on the edge of the area. He fluffed his attempted shot, which went to a teammate who got a toe on it and it then hit Mohamed Diame's ankle. How it then looped up and flew into the top corner was a mystery.

Fortunate Flick

http://y2u.be/MzINmOidnOM

Syrian striker Motaz Salhani scored just once for Jordanian side Al Wehdat during a brief spell with the club in 2014, but it was definitely a goal to remember. Sprinting toward the opposition goal, Salhani overran the through pass played to him by a team-mate and decided to try to get the ball in front of him with a flick of his boot behind his back. The unexpected result was a soaring volley from 40 yards, which sailed over the keeper and into the goal.

A STROKE OF LUCK FOR LITTLE PEA

PITCH PERFORMERS

Win or lose, supporters come to football matches to be entertained, and these goal scorers certainly didn't leave the fans disappointed.

▶ Do the Robot!

http://y2u.be/qBFQxqysGaA

At six-foot seven, Peter Crouch is one of the tallest players professional football has ever seen but the striker stood out from the crowd for a different reason in 2016. The lanky target man scored for England in a pre-World Cup friendly against Jamaica and promptly unveiled his "robot dance" celebration, which involved the Three Lions number nine mechanically moving his arms at the same time as gyrating his hips in front of the England fans and much to the amusement of his teammates.

◀ Masked Marvel

http://y2u.be/znYNhR2cSLg

Jonas Gutierrez scored 12 times for Newcastle United in over 200 appearances for the club between 2008 and 2015, but he's best remembered at St James' Park for his unique celebration, rather than the goals themselves. The eccentric Argentine midfielder always went out with a red Spider-Man mask stuffed into one of his socks and, every time he found the back of the net, he'd bring out the costume and run around pretending to be the Marvel superhero.

▼ Mocking the Manager

http://y2u.be/xnmAXUsoMAo

Prankster Jimmy Bullard came up with a clever celebration in 2009 by taking the mickey out of his Hull City boss, Phil Brown. The Tigers manager had famously given his team a half-time ticking off in full sight on the Eithad pitch the previous season so, when Bullard scored from the penalty spot, he gathered his teammates together and re-enacted the public dressing down, waving his finger at the players. Luckily for Bullard, Brown saw the funny side from the touchline.

▶ The Dentist's Chair

http://y2u.be/g0NT6aUwN8c

The England squad got into all sorts of trouble in the build-up to Euro 96 when it was revealed they'd been out late-night drinking on a Far East tour, pouring vodka down each other's throats while sat in a dentist's chair. Cue Paul Gascoigne's wild celebration after scoring against Scotland at Wembley – a cheeky recreation of the incident but this time with his teammates grabbing water bottles, rather than alcohol, to squirt into the midfielder's open mouth.

ON THE SPOT

A penalty is a moment of pure drama and, often, the attempt to score from 12 yards out is even more entertaining than anyone could have predicted.

▼ The Zaza Dance

http://y2u.be/bc_6t2zk5lw

The pressure of the penalty shootout can do funny things to a player, and that was definitely the case when Italy faced Germany in the quarter-finals of Euro 2016. There was nothing between the two teams after extra-time but the tension turned to tears of laughter when Simone Zaza stepped up to take Italy's second spot kick in the shootout. His hilarious run-up made him look like a prancing pony, but he didn't see the funny side after blasting his left-footed effort high over the crossbar.

The Tumble Tactic

http://y2u.be/RjLv6FJ20sI

Penalty takers are forever trying to distract or fool the goalkeeper and Maldives player Adey Ashadh came up with an ingenious way of confusing the custodian from the spot in an international against Afghanistan in 2014. Ashadh's run-up seemed normal enough at the start but, halfway to the ball, the forward "accidentally" fell over. He was back on his feet quick smart and promptly sent the bemused keeper the wrong way to score.

NOT A PENALTY SPECIALIST

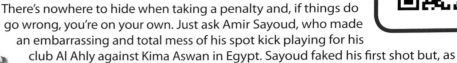

◄ Awful Amir

http://y2u.be/Nw6fABXDbl8

There's nowhere to hide when taking a penalty and, if things do go wrong, you're on your own. Just ask Amir Sayoud, who made an embarrassing and total mess of his spot kick playing for his club Al Ahly against Kima Aswan in Egypt. Sayoud faked his first shot but, as he prepared for his "real" attempt, he slipped and began to fall. Off balance and tumbling, his second effort was a weak one, which trickled apologetically into the arms of the goalkeeper. To complete his misery, Sayoud was then booked for trying to deceive the Aswan stopper.

A PATHETIC PEA-ROLLER

Ingenious Awana

http://y2u.be/xcSY-MVE6ZU

The element of surprise is one of the keys to a successful penalty, and there was no doubt Lebanon's goalkeeper was absolutely gobsmacked when the UAE's Theyab Awana beat him from the spot in 2011. Awana's ploy was certainly unusual, running toward goal in the usual fashion before, at the last minute, pirouetting and back-heeling the ball past the keeper.

Bounce of the Ball

http://y2u.be/dRN99zNjRHY

A football can sometimes do funny things, and it's safe to say no one could have predicted what was coming in Thailand in 2017 in the penalty shootout between Satri Angthong and Bangkok Sports Club. Angthong looked to have failed when one of their players smashed his spot kick against the crossbar, and the Bangkok keeper ran off in wild celebration. What he didn't know was that the ball had rather a lot of backspin and, after two bounces inside the area, it rolled into the back of the unguarded net.

Confusing the Keeper

http://y2u.be/mZEQrmpJHKg

One way to improve your chances of safely despatching a penalty is to send the goalkeeper the wrong way, which is exactly what Neymar did in 2011 when he was still a Santos player in Brazil. The playmaker jogged in and made to hit the ball but stopped his right boot at the last second. Unfortunately, the keeper had already fallen into the trap, diving to his right, and Neymar was now able to causally pass the ball into the opposite side of the goal.

FASHION FAILS

Modern footballers are millionaires but, as these embarrassing examples prove, money doesn't necessarily buy taste.

▶ Dani's Disasters

http://y2u.be/QZkv_C3YSXw

Dani Alves might have won more than a hundred international caps for Brazil, as well as plenty of silverware with Barcelona, Juventus and PSG during his club career, but the full-back is a serial fashion offender. It's safe to assume Alves likes to be noticed, judging by his choice of outrageous outfits over the years, and the Brazilian really surpassed himself when he once opted for a leather jacket complete with tiger-skin sleeves, white shirt, jeans and bow tie.

Skirting the Issue

http://y2u.be/CdOwoRgYYD0

David Beckham has always fancied himself as a bit of a trendsetter, but his fashion radar was definitely on the blink in 1998 when he stepped out in full view of the cameras wearing a black-and-white sarong. His man-skirt may well have been very comfy but, coupled as it was with a sleeveless black T-shirt, the overall effect was more desperate boy-band wannabe than style icon. The man himself, however, stands by his epic fashion fail. "Sarongs are great," he said. "That's one thing I never regret because I thought it looked great and I would still wear it now."

WE'D LIKE A WORD WITH DANI'S STYLIST

◀ Doesn't Suit You, Sir!

http://y2u.be/3_LIB0su5ZM

Millions of people tune in every year to watch the Ballon d'Or awards ceremony. The annual vote to crown the game's best player is a big deal but, when viewers turned on their TVs in 2013, they were stunned to see Lionel Messi show up in a terrible white polka-dot suit. His matching polka-dot bow tie had to be seen to be believed and left most fans wondering whether the Barcelona star had got dressed for the ceremony in the dark.

▼ Reds in White

http://y2u.be/vlKdPrTWUHs

Probably the worst ever choice of suits for the FA Cup final were worn by Liverpool in 1996, when their bright Giorgio Armani outfits made them a laughing stock at Wembley. "It was David James' fault we wore white suits," admitted embarrassed Reds striker Robbie Fowler after the giggling had finally stopped. "He's bigger than everyone so nobody questioned him and at the time he was an Armani model." Sadly for the Liverpool lads, their day only got worse when they were beaten 1-0 by Manchester United.

GETTING THE STRAWBERRIES AND CREAM LOOK

GAMES AND PASTIMES

As long as football remains popular, there'll always be a huge market for strange spin-offs and simulations of the beautiful game.

▶ Mechanical Madness

http://y2u.be/1h5147KLikU

Some scientists dream of a future in which robots are able to do anything and everything humans can do, so it was probably only a matter of time before they had a crack at creating miniature, mechanical footballers. Their creations can be seen in action every year at the Robo Cup but, if you watch the clip, you'll see that their robots' main skill is taking a dive, rather than banging the ball into the top corner.

Game Plan

http://y2u.be/p06C3_umT9g

Sending scouts all over the world to watch players can be an expensive business and, in 2008, Premier League side Everton decided to save themselves some cash when they signed a deal with the makers of the Football Manager video game, giving the club exclusive access to a database of more than 370,000 players in 50 different countries. The clever idea was to identify the best unknown and obscure players on the game and only then despatch someone to actually watch them in action.

▶ Toilet Target

http://y2u.be/qnVPsE46lMY

Going to the gents suddenly got more a little bit more interesting for football fanatics in 2007 when a German company unveiled their unusual new product – the "Klo-Kicker". A miniature plastic goal that sits inside a urinal, it encouraged men to aim for the back of the net when nature called. The tiny football in the middle of the goal even changed colour from red to white if you were accurate enough with your "shot".

APPEALING TO A BROAD-ER AUDIENCE

◀ Girl Power

http://y2u.be/xkxpVnailJM

Table football was invented by an Englishman by the name of Harold Searles Thornton back in the 1920s and, although the digital age has stolen some of the game's thunder, it's still a big hit with football lovers all over the world. In 2009, the game was given a serious makeover when designers decided to replace the iconic players with rows of Barbie dolls. The new figures certainly looked pretty in pink but whether table football and high heels are the best combination is debatable.

▶ Shankly's Subbuteo

http://y2u.be/SK2ILHJtP-Y

Legend has it that Liverpool manager Bill Shankly once used a Subbuteo set in a pre-match team talk to prepare his side for a game against arch rivals Manchester United, and this picture proves the Anfield icon was definitely a fan of the classic game. He wasn't, though, the only one: the Subbuteo World Cup was first played in 1987 and is still held today, while the English Subbuteo Football Association has more than 800 followers on its Facebook page.

▶ We See You

http://y2u.be/2z7djMG6G7M

Borussia Dortmund's fans are well known for their phenomenal tifo choreography, and the club's famous Yellow Wall was at its best before the Champions League quarterfinal against Malaga in 2013. An intimidating figure sporting binoculars greeted the teams as they walked out on to the pitch, rising above a banner that read: "On the trail of the lost cup". The frightening composition did the trick too, as Dortmund secured a late victory thanks to a stoppage-time winner.

HE'S BEHIND YOU!

KIT SHOCKERS

Replica shirt sales are big business these days, with the big clubs spending millions on cutting-edge designs, but you probably couldn't give away these horrendous strips.

◀ Design Flaw

http://y2u.be/Pk-k2DW65c8

Mexico's first-choice goalkeeper for much of the 1990s, Jorge Campos, also fancied himself as something of a fashionista and insisted on designing his own kit. The result was a series of horrendous and painfully bright shirts that were guaranteed to induce a blinding headache in any opposition player or fan foolish enough to look in Campos's direction for more than a minute.

▶ In the Pink

http://y2u.be/jbgmQ-0_gbY

Pink is not a colour that is traditionally associated with the beautiful game, but that didn't stop Everton deciding it would be the perfect colour for their away strip for the 2010–11 Premier League season. Finished off with a couple of elephants on the front and the name of a Thai drinks company, the shirts were certainly eye catching but didn't do the team any particular favours on the pitch, as the Toffees eventually finished seventh in the table, one place below arch rivals Liverpool.

Tiger Tragedy

http://y2u.be/kQf63Ffk62g

Hull City are also known as the Tigers and it was, of course, only a matter of time before some clever designer hit on the idea of commemorating the nickname in the form of a new shirt. The new kit was duly unveiled ahead of the 1993–94 season and featured swirling orange and black stripes to mimic a tiger's skin but, rather than conjuring images of the majestic big cat, the shirt looked like a hyperactive five-year-old had been unleashed on a paint set.

▼ Keeper Catastrophe

http://y2u.be/3EiE7eLWI_M

England's pristine white shirt is famous across the football world, but anyone unlucky to have seen the Three Lions goalkeeper's kit in 1995 and 1996 is probably still trying to erase the image from their minds. Most infamously worn by David Seaman in the semi-final of Euro 96 against Germany at Wembley, the shirt was a mental mash-up of purple, green, yellow and red, which sadly failed to dazzle the German players enough to make them miss in a dramatic penalty shootout.

THE GOLDEN AGE OF AWFUL KITS

Tassel Hassle

http://y2u.be/GTonZ3U-4-Q

America hasn't always "got" football, and never was that sporting misunderstanding more evident than when a team called the Colorado Caribous took to the field in 1978 in a horrendous white, beige and black kit, complete with hilarious leather tassels around the middle. The top looked more like a prop from a low-budget western than a football shirt, and it obviously didn't do the Colorado players any favours either, as the team slumped to 22 defeats and was disbanded at the end of the season.

DUGOUT CAPERS

The action is usually out on the pitch but, occasionally, the best entertainment during a match can actually be seen on the sidelines.

HOSTILE TERRITORY

▲ Water, Water Everywhere!

http://y2u.be/u4lMbSr2ZYk

Football's all about kicking a ball and, if angry Arsène Wenger had stuck to this simple rule in 2009, the Arsenal manager wouldn't have found himself in the stands. The Frenchman was angry after his side had a goal disallowed against Manchester United at Old Trafford, and he took his frustration out on an innocent water bottle in his technical area, launching it several feet into the area. Referee Mike Dean was not impressed and sent him to the stands, resulting in Wenger comically clambering over the top of the visitors' dug-out to watch the last few seconds of the match.

▶ It's My Ball!

http://y2u.be/6JM0niOycb0

Former Man City manager Roberto Mancini was normally a pretty calm guy, but the angry Italian completely lost the plot during a Premier League clash with Everton in 2010, body slamming opposite number David Moyes in his technical area after the Scot refused to give the ball back. Mancini's unexpected attack on Moyes for the missing ball worked a treat, but he wasn't smiling for long, as referee Peter Walton told them to both grow up and sent the pair to the stands.

HANDBAGS AT DAWN

▲ Sleepy Head

http://y2u.be/TGIrcMV53Bs

It's understandable when substitutes lose interest in a game, especially when they think they've got no chance of getting on the pitch. Falling asleep in the dugout, however, is totally unacceptable, but that didn't stop Real Madrid's Julien Faubert grabbing 40 winks during his 3-2 win against Villarreal in Spain in 2009. Unluckily for Faubert, his quick kip was caught on camera and, unsurprisingly, he was quickly sent packing by Madrid after making just two appearances for the club.

Dugout Imposter

http://y2u.be/YEXv77m1s-Y

Ticketless Republic of Ireland fan Conor Cunningham was so desperate to watch his side's crucial clash with Estonia in Tallinn in 2011, that he decided he'd try a bit of theft and then impersonation to watch the match. First, the 27-year-old stole an Estonian team tracksuit and, after waking past security guards posing as one of the substitutes, he then calmly sat next to Estonian manager Tarmo Ruutli. Cunningham recorded the game on his mobile phone but was eventually rumbled by stewards and sent packing.

TOP OF THE POPS

Plenty of players enjoy a sing-song in the dressing room, but some just can't resist sharing their musical talents with a wider audience.

◀ Rocking Roque

http://y2u.be/GW-ojhMZty4

Some players' involvement in recording a song can be very brief indeed, and they don't come any shorter than Roque Santa Cruz's contribution to 2004 heavy-metal tune "Ich Roque", written by German group Sportfreunde Stiller. All the Paraguay striker had to do was say "Ich roque" (I rock) at the start of the chorus and leave the rest of the work to the band for one of the most one-sided musical collaborations ever.

▶ Language Barrier

http://y2u.be/3X8ocYRXOAU

When he wasn't going on strike, sulking or demanding yet another transfer, Argentina striker Carlos Tevez liked to get together with his brother, Diego, and front their band, called Piola Vago. The group's biggest hit – "Lose Control" – charted in Argentina, but the forward admitted he didn't bother to share his Spanish tunes with former Man United teammates. "Here it's all hip-hop, all in English, so they don't understand a thing," he said. "They want to hear it, they ask me but I say no to them."

▶ Bum Rap

http://y2u.be/6PhRq0UxF74

Plenty of players have a nickname in the dressing room, but USA striker Clint Dempsey decided to adopt the alias of "Deuce" when he recorded a single for Nike in the build-up to the 2006 World Cup in Germany. Performing alongside rappers XO and Big Hawk, Dempsey sang his heart out on the song "Don't Tread", but the song failed to inspire the American team, as they headed home early after failing to win any of their group-stage games at the tournament.

Musical Morte

http://y2u.be/EpoaVD6KOvI

With his bleached-blond hair and youthful good looks, Norwegian midfielder Morte Ganst Pedersen already looked like a member of a boy band and, after years of jokes, he decided to call everyone's bluff and actually join one. Teaming up with footballers from the Norwegian Premier League, Pedersen became part of a group that decided to call themselves The Players and released a track called "This Is for Real". Unbelievably, the song became a big hit across Scandinavia.

▶ Wonder of Waddle

http://y2u.be/4ct5puqTSi0

The king of the mullet, Chris Waddle, reached Number 20 in the UK charts in 1987 when he released "Diamond Lights" with Spurs teammate and future England manager Glenn Hoddle, but the winger had a second stab at pop stardom in France after he signed for Marseille in 1989, recording "We've Got A Feeling" with team-mate Basil Boli. Cartoon zebras and the Houses of Parliament featured heavily in the video but exactly what feeling the two players were having remains a mystery.

SUPER SKILLS

Incredible tricks and fantastic flicks that really have to be seen to be believed.

▲ Back Pass

http://y2u.be/BaKSFeK3EXo

There's pretty much nothing Cristiano Ronaldo can't do with a football, and his breathtaking trick playing for Real Madrid against Real Sociedad in Spain in 2011 was something really out of this world. Drifting out toward the touchline, the Portuguese player beat his defender with an outrageous pass to himself off his own back, deflecting the ball over the head of the stunned Sociedad player before spinning around his marker and collecting possession.

CRISTIANO GOT BACK

Pele's Swerve

http://y2u.be/-UzRsvCsC4c

Some of the best tricks don't even involve touching the football, and one of the most famous was Pele's genius swerve during Brazil's World Cup clash with Uruguay in 1970. Pele was put clean through, but the goalkeeper came rushing out and, rather than try to take it around him, the Brazilian legend ran across the stopper but let the ball keep rolling in the opposite direction. It worked a treat, and he picked up the ball in the penalty area, with the goalkeeper completely stranded.

▶ Robinho's Rainbow

http://y2u.be/UQLXjebbBKg

Good players keep their eye on the ball when they're defending, but that's easier said than done when you're up against a world-class talent. Just ask Alexis Sanchez, who was left looking very silly indeed playing for Barcelona against AC Milan in 2013 when he tried to tackle Robinho but was completely beaten by the Brazilian's remarkable rainbow flick, which sailed over his head before he knew what was even happening.

GIROUD'S STING IN THE TAIL

◀ Awesome Oliver

http://y2u.be/yH85k6uEcHc

French striker Olivier Giroud has scored more than a century of goals for Arsenal since signing for the club in 2012, and the pick of the bunch has to be his sensational scorpion kick for the Gunners against Crystal Palace in 2017. The forward bust a gut to get into the area and on the end of Alexis Sanchez's cross, and then left the crowd speechless with a fabulous flick from behind his back to send the ball flying into the top corner.

67

CRAZY CELEBRATIONS

There's no better feeling in football than finding the back of the net, but it does sometimes make the goal scorer react rather strangely.

▶ That's Pants

http://y2u.be/gVwj91iKxbs

Some players just can't resist the urge to undress when they score a goal, but Montenegro star Mirko Vucinic decided peeling off his shirt just wasn't enough in 2010 after finding the back of the net against Switzerland. Instead the Roma striker decided to whip off his shorts in celebration, pop them onto his head and run around the pitch in his underwear like some kind of a crazed and slightly indecent lunatic.

WHY THE Y-FRONTS?

◀ Quack Quack

http://y2u.be/Y4eKo5lg-p4

The most famous thing about the little Buckinghamshire town of Aylesbury used to be the breed of duck named after it and, in 1995, the local team decided to pay tribute to the town's feathered friend when they unveiled their brilliant "duck waddling" celebration. The part-timers loved their wacky waddle so much they even performed their famous routine after being knocked out of the FA Cup by Queens Park Rangers.

Diving German

http://y2u.be/-Mikgy19u20

Some people say Germans don't have a sense of humour, but Jurgen Klinsmann proved them wrong during his spells with Spurs in the 1990s. The striker was criticized for diving and, to prove he saw the funny side of things, Klinsmann performed a "splash dive" every time he scored. He unveiled his tongue-in-cheek celebration for the first time after netting against Sheffield Wednesday in 1994 and was joined by half of the Spurs side in what was a hilarious and choreographed routine.

▼ Using Your Head

http://y2u.be/mvp5ExhhX7M

Brazilian Neymar is well known for his flamboyance and the PSG superstar definitely lived up to his reputation in early 2018 after scoring in a cup quarter-final clash against Amiens. Rather than a quick cuddle with his teammates or a victory salute to the PSG faithful, Neymar whipped off one of his boots and balance it on his head in celebration. His sponsors Nike were particularly happy as pictures of their footwear on top of the Brazilian's bonce were seen all over the world.

▲ A Dog's Life

http://y2u.be/0_mwyGKBSwI

You can't always account for taste, and there's no denying Nigerian striker Finidi George went barking mad after scoring a wonderful breakaway goal for his country against Greece in the 1994 World Cup finals. After his spectacular score, George ran toward the nearest corner flag. Nothing seemed out of the ordinary until the former Ajax star then unexpectedly got down onto his hands and knees and crawled around like a dog, before raising his back leg and pretending to urinate on the grass.

WATCH OUT FOR THE STUDS!

HANDS OFF!

Football is predominantly played with the feet, but sometimes players just can't resist the temptation to get their hands on the ball.

◀ Scholes Rumbled

http://y2u.be/kme2xaGi49A

A sly handball in the area can so often result in a goal with the referee none the wiser as the "scorer" celebrates. It was, however, the complete opposite for Manchester United's Paul Scholes when he decided to smack the ball into the net with his right hand in a Champions League clash against Zenit St Petersburg in 2008. The problem was Scholes wasn't sneaky enough, rising above the defenders and then clearly slapping the ball into the back of the net like a volleyball player. The referee disallowed it and showed the United midfielder a second yellow for his obvious attempt to pull a fast one.

NOT QUITE THE "HAND OF GOD"

▶ Gormless Ghezzal

http://y2u.be/9R_w5_Wtybw

The 2010 World Cup in South Africa saw one of the most unintentionally comical and idiotic uses of the hand when Algeria's Abdelkader Ghezzal temporarily lost his marbles and got himself sent off. Ghezzal came off the bench against Slovenia in the 58th minute and, within 48 seconds, got himself booked for shirt pulling. But worse was to come 15 minutes later when Ghezzal leaped into the air to bring down a high pass, thrusting his right arm out. The inevitable red card almost flew out of the referee's pocket and, within six minutes, Slovenia scored the winner against the depleted Africans.

SNEAKY SUAREZ SAVES

▲ Ghana Robbed

http://y2u.be/a4B0_SI2RHU

Uruguay's Luis Suarez wrote his name into World Cup history for all the wrong reasons in South Africa in 2010 when he single-handedly sent Ghana crashing out of the tournament. The quarter-final between the two teams was locked at 1-1 in the dying seconds of normal time when Ghana's Dominic Adiyah headed what appeared certain to be a dramatic winner. Suarez, however, had other ideas and punched the ball away. A red card and penalty followed but Asamoah Gyan could not convert for the Africans and Uruguay eventually triumphed in a penalty shootout. Suarez was banned for the semi-final but, if there was ever a case of the punishment not fitting the crime, that was it.

▶ Ronaldo's Slam Dunk

http://y2u.be/9bSDurpclu4

Cristiano Ronaldo has produced countless moments of magic during his career, but his bizarre leap and catch in Real Madrid's Champions League game with Man City in 2016 definitely wasn't one of them. Lurking in the six-yard box, the Portuguese star jumped to meet a cross but mistimed it badly and ended up catching the ball with both hands and throwing it into the back of the net. Ronaldo thought it was hilarious, but the City players were definitely not amused.

PUMPED-UP FANS

If a game isn't particularly inspiring, fans can have to take matters into their own hands. From blow-up toys to epic choreography, sometimes the real action can be in the stands.

▼ Fantastic Fruit

http://y2u.be/oTmaXOcwdRo

The inflatable craze was a phenomenon that swept British football in the late 1980s and early 1990s, and it all began when Manchester City faced West Brom in 1988. During the game, the waggish City fans began chanting for "Imre Banana" to come off the bench, even though his real name was Imre Varadi, but the nickname stuck and the City supporters decided to bring inflatable bananas to every game after that, paving the way for fans up and down the country to follow suit with their own array of comedy blow-ups.

Co-ordinated Koreans

http://y2u.be/czmxO1qeWC0

Type "human jumbotron" into any search engine and you'll find images of the most incredible, choreographed routines performed by Korean football fans, which will take your breath away. Thousands of supporters take part, holding different coloured and patterned boards or wearing contrasting clothing. They move together with incredible co-ordination to create massive images from the stands. Think giant human video screen and you're getting close.

VERY A-PEEL-ING

▲ Beach Ball Gaffe

http://y2u.be/rPKPZchZitg

As a rule of thumb, inflatables should remain with the supporters in the stands, and the consequences of a stray blow-up drifting onto the pitch can be disastrous. And quite funny. One such unfortunate incident occurred during Sunderland's clash with Liverpool at the Stadium of Light in 2009, when an inflatable beach ball smuggled in by the visiting fans was thrown onto the pitch just as Darren Bent shot at goal. Sadly for Liverpool, the "real" ball took a wicked deflection off the air-filled impostor, deceiving goalkeeper Pepe Reina, and hit the back of the net.

▲ Happy Harry

http://y2u.be/Bri136qRGAo

Grimsby fans were quick to jump on the inflatable bandwagon, and they ensured that their blow-up mascots had a local flavour, opting for a blow-up "Harry the Haddock", to reflect the town's fishing industry. Thousands of the four-foot long fish were spotted at Mariners' games and, although more recently Grimsby fans have added more items to their repertoire, this 2015 clip from their visit to Barnet proves they still can't get enough of their inflatable props.

ADVERT FOR THE GAME

Advertisers are always looking for famous folk to help flog their products and, unfortunately, that sometimes results in footballers appearing in comical commercials.

▶The Shower Scene

http://y2u.be/Xf-4Gbqyni4

Famed for his tight bubble perm and celebrity lifestyle, Kevin Keegan was something of a trailblazer as a player in the 1970s and 1980s, but probably blazed just a bit too much when he appeared in an advert for Brut aftershave with heavyweight boxer Henry Cooper. The commercial featured the two greats enjoying a workout but things got a little steamy when they retreated to the shower to joke about who liked the manly smell of Brut the best. Things really bottomed out when Cooper removed his towel to throw it at Kev.

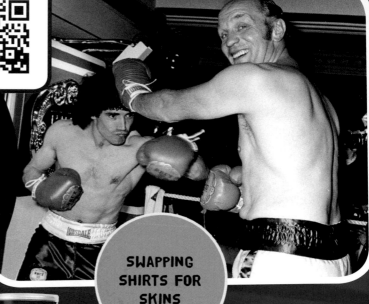

SWAPPING SHIRTS FOR SKINS

▶ Crunchy Kickabout

http://y2u.be/usjJjP3Mc9Y

One of the golden rules of adverts featuring footballers is that the players must be shown showcasing their silky skills and tricks, no matter what they're actually promoting. Step forward the embarrassed quartet of French striker Nicolas Anelka, Dutch forward Dirk Kuyt, Spanish midfielder Cesc Fabregas and England target man Peter Crouch kicking around an empty tin of Pringles for a 2010 TV ad that proved, once and for all, that footballers can't act but that they are rather good at crisp-based keepie-up.

Dog Days

http://y2u.be/Oy9qKiApmY0

Some players advertise top-of-the range clothes brands, luxury aftershaves or ridiculously expensive watches. Some aren't quite so lucky, and former Liverpool and Chelsea striker Fernando Torres fell into that category after he unwisely agreed to appear in a truly awful TV advert in his native Spain for a dog-training school. It was the definition of low-rent, and Torres' made a right dogs' dinner of the acting, most people agreeing he was upstaged by a rather talented Alsatian.

◀ Wright Gets It All Wrong

http://y2u.be/AN3gTKTQgFk

Dancing in public – let alone in front of the cameras – is always a risky business, and former Arsenal and England striker Ian Wright should definitely have thought twice before he agreed to make a complete fool of himself and advertise Chicken Tonight cooking sauce. Getting dressed up in a smoking jacket and cravat was bad enough but Wright's bizarre "chicken dance" halfway through the awful advert had the audience desperately reaching for their remotes.

▶ Chemical Cash

http://y2u.be/s32uMiY0HGY

There aren't many men who would happily admit to even their closest friends that they needed extra "help" in the trouser department, but most men aren't Pele, who became the face of Viagra in 2005. The Brazil legend told anyone who'd listen, in a series of commercials, about the wonders of the new drug, banking millions in the process, while embarrassed men of a certain age suddenly rushed to their local chemist.

Love Life To the Fullest

Pelé

75

INTERVIEW FUNNIES

Talking to the media is part and parcel of life as a footballer or manager, and sometimes their dealings with the press can be as entertaining as what happens out on the pitch.

▶ Pop the Kettle On!

http://y2u.be/9yMOW2u2A2Y

The magic of the FA Cup comes when lower-league minnows get the chance to play the big boys from the Premier League, and so it was in 2016 when League Two Exeter City entertained Liverpool at St James' Park. Reds boss Jurgen Klopp gave the BBC a pre-match interview and nothing initially seemed out of the ordinary until the camera panned left to reveal that, rather than a plush media room, the Liverpool manager was actually standing in the tiny Exeter tea room, right next to the kettle and sink.

Ronaldo Goes AWOL

http://y2u.be/ZfXyEEw9U-0

The relationship between players and football journalists isn't always a happy one, and it took a turn for the worst in 2016 when Cristiano Ronaldo got the hump after a Spanish reporter asked him about a recent goal drought. Much annoyed shrugging of shoulders from the Portuguese superstar followed, but the Real Madrid star wasn't finished and, after giving the hack the evil eye, he picked up his tracksuit top and stormed out of the press conference without another word.

◄ Cake Break

http://y2u.be/vNThMAnIZlc

Given that Antonio Conte's first language isn't English, his post-match press conferences as Chelsea manager are usually pretty engaging. His meet with the media after his team had played Leicester City in 2016, however, was even more entertaining than usual when the hungry Italian spied a reporter tucking into a delicious-looking slice of sponge cake and, temporarily halting proceedings, asked the journalist if he could have a taste for himself. The reporter obliged and Conte helped himself.

▼ Casillas's Kiss

http://y2u.be/7d0klZsZOXk

Winning the World Cup is an emotional experience, and Spain goalkeeper Iker Casillas was visibly moved after his team were crowned world champions in South Africa in 2010. Speaking to a female reporter, the then Real Madrid star struggled to get his words out and, on the verge of tears, decided the best way to express himself was to kiss the journalist live on air. Luckily for him, Sara Carbonero just happened to be his girlfriend, and the couple got married six years later.

A VERY INTIMATE INTERVIEW

HITTING THE DECK

The beautiful game is supposed to be played standing up but, sadly, there have always been some football folk who just can't seem to stay upright.

▶ The Anti-dive

http://y2u.be/ZUrcX6kpkU0

Not all footballers are cheats and, back in 1997, Robbie Fowler suddenly had an attack of conscience after he fell over Arsenal goalkeeper David Seaman to win a controversial penalty. Racked by guilt at his own skulduggery, the Liverpool striker begged referee Gerald Ashby not to award his side the spot kick. Despite his confession, the official forced Liverpool to take the penalty and, although Fowler's kick was saved, Jason McAteer banged in the rebound. It was win-win for the Scouser, though, when he was later handed a Fair Play Award by UEFA.

▶ Meier's Madness

http://y2u.be/ff7RPnWRkIE

Managers are meant to set a good example to their players, but Duisburg boss Norbert Meier did the complete opposite in 2005 when his side faced Bundesliga rivals Cologne. The incident began when the gaffer stopped opposition midfielder Albert Streit from taking a quick throw-in and the pair squared up to each other. Meier then gave Streit the gentlest of headbutts and, despite there being no lasting damage done to either man, both then comically threw themselves backward and down onto the pitch.

The Off-balance Official

http://y2u.be/eHGYKW57QPE

Play-acting is clearly a bug that's catching in Brazil, and even the referees aren't immune from it. During a Fourth Division clash between Operario and Mirassol in 2011, referee Rodrigo Nunes de Sa brandished a straight red card to a Mirassol man, who reacted by moving his head toward the man in black. After gently making contact, the official threw himself backward and hit the deck like he had just been shot by a sniper. Players from both sides didn't like what they saw and riot police were summoned to keep the angry mob at bay.

Rossi Rumbled

http://y2u.be/lufnlu5842w

The art of a convincing dive is to throw yourself to the turf when you're actually near an opponent to create the illusion of a foul. Sadly, Italy's Daniele de Rossi didn't seem to know this, judging by his ridiculous fall during the Azzurri's 2010 World Cup showdown with Paraguay. There was no one near the midfielder when he suddenly tumbled just outside the box and, for once, the referee agreed, waving away the Italian's angry but ridiculous calls for a free kick.

Crafty Carrasco

http://y2u.be/aNgNy5IbwOc

Some dives are more inventive than others, and one hilarious example of going down for no good reason came in Chile's U-20s fixture with Ecuador in 2011. Our culprit was Chilean Bryan Carrasco, who ambled up to mark one of the opposition from a throw-in and, when he thought no one was looking, grabbed the player's hand and punched himself in the face with it. Cue a theatrical dive, which got him the free kick he was hoping for but was also caught by the cameras.

A+ FOR ACTING

MAD MANAGERS

The boss is the man in charge, the one who's supposed to set an example, but the pressures of the job can sometimes make them do crazy things.

▼ Going Loco

http://y2u.be/IlUtklMb7wQ

Nicknamed "El Loco" (or "the Crazy One"), Argentinean coach Marcelo Bielsa proved over the years that there is genuine method to his obvious madness. Among his crazy ideas, he likes to make his defenders and strikers train at different places at different times and is also happy to conduct four-hour press conferences. Bielsa was also the Argentina manager for the 2002 World Cup and, as preparation for the tournament, ordered his players to watch 700 football DVDs before booking them into the worst hotel he could find.

COVER UP CLOUGHY!

▶ Old Big Head

http://y2u.be/E_LUGY_ptGA

The late, great Brian Clough was one of the best managers English football has ever produced, but he was also slightly bonkers. Dubbed "Old Big Head" because of his ridiculous self-confidence, Cloughie was a journalist's dream for rattling off quotes like, "I wouldn't say I was the best manager in the business but I was in the top one," and, "Rome wasn't built in a day but I wasn't on that particular job." He also famously ordered his Nottingham Forest players to have a beer on the bus on the way to the 1979 European Cup final.

▼ Dangerous Diego

http://y2u.be/JDwgYDMdA3k

Atletico Madrid boss Diego Simeone could start a fight in an empty room and he was at his crazy worst during his team's 2014 Champions League final against Real Madrid. The Argentine took exception to the way Raphael Varane celebrated after Real had scored in the penalty shootout, and he launched an insane one-man pitch invasion and had to be repeatedly held back by the referee as he furiously tried to get to the defender. He was eventually escorted off the pitch after one of the game's most unbelievable managerial meltdowns.

DON'T MESS WITH DIEGO

◄ Jurgen Loses It

http://y2u.be/aZncYO0zjHg

Liverpool boss Jurgen Klopp is known as a bit of a joker but, like most managers, he's got a nasty side. Just ask the poor fourth official who was unlucky enough to be standing next to the German during a Champions League game between Napoli and Borussia Dortmund. Klopp didn't like something he'd seen out on the pitch, and the look on his face as he confronted the petrified official was one of the most terrifying images you're ever likely to see on a touchline.

81

EXTREME KEEPIE-UPPIE

Anyone who likes football enjoys a bit of keepie-uppie, but this lot simply can't stand to ever see the ball hit the ground.

▼ Marathon Man

http://y2u.be/Eof6HZ-EpPc

The 26 miles and 385 yards of the London marathon are the ultimate test of endurance and stamina but, back in 2011, England's John Farnworth decided to make the race even more of a challenge by attempting to juggle a football along the entire distance of the famous course in the capital. Once doctors had established that Farnworth wasn't mad, he set off on his on his bizarre mission and finished the race in an impressive 12 hours and 15 minutes.

Awesome Ash

http://y2u.be/zrJTO5DdYhE

An interesting version of keepie-uppie is lying on your back and keeping the ball in the air with only the soles of your feet. Ash Randall is a master of the skill and, in 2010, he tried to set the record for the most touches of a ball in one minute. The Cardiff City fan began his attempt during half-time of the Bluebirds league game with Watford and was all smiles after 60 action-packed seconds, setting an impressive new world record of 220 horizontal keepie-uppies.

JUGGLING GENIUS

▶ Streets of London

http://y2u.be/BsRN-8WABY0

Dan Magness is addicted to keepie-uppie and, not content with setting the record for the longest time keeping the ball in the air, he's also the record holder for the longest distance covered while juggling. In 2010, the incredible Englishman started at Fulham's Craven Cottage ground and finished at Tottenham's White Hart Lane to set his magical milestone, covering an unbelievable 36 miles of the streets of London without once letting the ball hit the pavement.

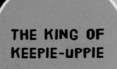
THE KING OF KEEPIE-UPPIE

Dan Magness
www.danmagness.com

The Need for Speed

http://y2u.be/2IPdKjtBxRU

Keepie-uppie normally tends to slow down the person juggling the ball, but Englishman Laurent Kelly decided to buck the trend in 2015 when he attempted to set a new world record for the fastest ever 400 metres while keeping the ball airborne. He headed to the nearest athletics track and was all smiles when the stopwatch confirmed he'd done his lap in a record 2 minutes and 8.82 seconds.

The Big Climb

http://y2u.be/oFA0JLWgVGY

It takes imagination to think of new and innovative keepie-up challenges, and Switzerland's Paul Sahli definitely had his thinking cap on when he wondered exactly how many steps of a ladder he could climb while juggling a football. The only way to find out was to grab the nearest ladder and ball and give it a whirl, with Sahli eventually managing to climb 111 steps without dropping the ball before vertigo got the better of him.

83

MARATHON

▼ Over the Net!

http://y2u.be/tCiT7Ba5OdM

Football's answer to volleyball, "Sepak Takraw" is a popular game in Malaysia and Thailand that dates back 600 years and, although you'll need a net to play, there are definitely no goalkeepers. The sport sees two teams of three players line up on a pitch that roughly the same size as a badminton court and kick, volley and head a small ball over a 1.5-metre net. With points and sets, the scoring system is similar to tennis but with less rackets and far fewer arguments with the umpires.

THAT'S GOTTA HURT

Football's a physical game and, in the heat of battle, players are always in danger of getting damaged. The results can be truly eye-watering.

▶ Koutris Catastrophe

http://y2u.be/rF_3yYredu4

It just wasn't Leonardo Koutris's day when his club, Ergotelis, faced Larissa in a Greek league match in 2005. The midfielder was body slammed on the edge of the area by a defender and went down painfully, clutching his side, but worse was to follow when the two stretcher bearers turned up. The part-time medics first threw him clumsily onto the stretcher, despite his protests, and, as they made their way to the sidelines, they twice stumbled and dropped the poor player back onto the pitch.

MEDICAL MELTDOWN IN GREECE

Babb Busted

http://y2u.be/dONtFBuCztM

Defenders hate conceding goals and Liverpool centre half Phil Babb certainly went to eye-watering extremes to stop Chelsea scoring in a Premier League clash at Anfield back in 1998. Striker Pierluigi Casiraghi went around Reds goalkeeper David James and slid the ball toward goal. Babb slid desperately across the grass to intercept but, with his legs spread, he couldn't stop himself as the post loomed and he smacked into the woodwork, groin first. The doctor rushed on, while every male supporter in the ground winced in sympathy.

Savage Blow

http://y2u.be/1SLZh_UWzpE

Danger can lurk in the most unlikely of places on a football pitch, and Leicester City's Robbie Savage certainly wasn't expecting to be poleaxed by referee Matt Messias during his side's 1993 clash with Newcastle. Messias flung his arm out to indicate a foul but had no idea the Foxes star was jogging up behind him and smashed the unlucky midfielder square in the face with his right elbow. Savage was probably not amused as he slumped to the floor, but Newcastle's Alan Shearer thought it was hilarious, showing Messias his own red card for the unprovoked attack.

◄ Tooth Ache

http://y2u.be/W96AeFFPWIM

Gumshields are usually worn by rugby players, but Dutch defender Demy de Zeeuw must have wished he'd had some dental protection in his side's World Cup semi-final with Uruguay in Cape Town in 2010. The Dutchman went for a clearing header but was smashed in the face by the boot of Martin Caceres, who was attempting a bicycle kick, and de Zeeuw hit the deck, unconscious. He was rushed to hospital with a suspected broken jaw, while Caceres was lucky to escape with only a yellow card.

A DENTAL DISASTER

87

EXTREME WEATHER

The beautiful game is played outdoors and that means players, fans and matches are frequently at the mercy of Mother Nature.

▶ Wind of Change

http://y2u.be/JOgh8GMeo4M

Sadly, footballers occasionally have to duck and dive to avoid various objects thrown by idiots in the crowd, but the players of the Black Leopards and Orlando Pirates in South Africa were faced by a far bigger flying threat in 2007 when a storm suddenly started blowing the advertising hoardings at Ellis Park onto the pitch. The game was only five minutes old when the huge gust of wind flung the boards around, and players from both sides – as well as the referee – needed medical attention for their injuries.

Is There Anybody Out There?

http://y2u.be/6tRyD4al2no

A healthy crowd of 63,499 squeezed into St James' Park for the FA Cup clash between defending champions Newcastle United and Swansea City back in 1953, but the two sets of fans only saw eight minutes of action before the game was abandoned. The culprit was a thick, impenetrable layer of fog that came out of nowhere. When the referee realized he had absolutely no idea how many players were on the pitch, he blew his whistle and groped his way back to the tunnel.

The Big Freeze

http://y2u.be/C_v2c-8_BS4

Anyone who plays football in Iceland has to get used to the cold pretty quickly. The country is on the edge of the Arctic Circle and freezing conditions are par for the course. The league match between Breiðablik and Fram in 2017 was something else, as an Arctic storm blew across the pitch and made football almost impossible. The referee, however, still insisted on 70 minutes of action before finally accepting that the snow, gale-force winds and lack of visibility were too much, even for Iceland's hardiest players.

▲ Eye of the Storm

http://y2u.be/HfzNl9cFde4

They say a little bit of rain never hurt anyone but, when it comes with terrifying bolts of lightning and enormous claps of thunder, it's best not to take any chances. At least that's what UEFA bosses decided when an apocalyptic storm engulfed the Donbass Arena in Donetsk just moments after kick-off between Ukraine and France at Euro 2012. The players ran for cover in the dressing rooms, while soaked supporters huddled together at the back of the stands for shelter. After a 55-minute delay, the match resumed as the skies thankfully cleared.

▼ Hail Mary!

http://y2u.be/zZ_CdPywd84

Belgium's international friendly with Tunisia in Brussels in 2014 was meant to be part of the side's World Cup warm-up, but things didn't exactly go according to plan when the game was temporarily abandoned in the first half. The problem at the Stade Roi Baudouin was a sudden downpour of giant hailstones, which could have done the players serious damage, and the referee sensibly decided it would be safer for everyone to scarper back to the dressing rooms.

▶ Swimming Lessons

http://y2u.be/VzLvf2yGCJQ

Many games have had to contend with the odd rain shower, but São Paulo's match with Palmeiras in 2011 witnessed such a torrential downpour that the fans were literally swimming in the water-filled concrete stands of the Morumbi Stadium before kick-off. Rivers of water were cascading down through the terraces but, amazingly, the match still went ahead after a 70-minute delay – only for another interruption in the second half when the water got into the electrics and caused a floodlight failure.

TIME FOR A SWIM IN SAO PAOLO

KEEP OFF THE PITCH!

Making a dash for it onto the sacred turf can land you in hot water with the law, but sometimes it can actually be worth the risk.

SIGN ON THE STRIPED LINE

◀ Audacious Argentine

http://y2u.be/IGYT-J33Oy8

Signed football memorabilia is big business these days, and one fan came up with a very unusual way of getting the shirt of his dreams in 2014 when Argentina were playing in a friendly in Hong Kong. The supporter was wearing an Argentina top and was so desperate to have Lionel Messi's signature on it that he ran on the pitch and was absolutely stunned when the Barcelona superstar agreed to give him his autograph. Exactly where Messi got the big black marker pen to do the job is unclear.

Get In!

http://y2u.be/7MfO_ZEyRvU

A lot of the uninvited fans who get onto the pitch are frustrated footballers, and that was definitely the case when two Barnsley supporters jumped over the advertising hoardings behind the goal during their team's match against Man United in 2009. United keeper Ben Foster was about to take a goal kick, only for one of the naughty fans to unexpectedly steal the ball from in front of him and pass it – via a lucky deflection off Foster's leg – to his mate, who then scored with what was a cracking volley.

Two Goals, One Equalizer

http://y2u.be/SBlDKoswSFw

A Honduran league fixture between Olimpia and Motagua in 2017 was the scene for one of the most bizarre and controversial pitch invasions of recent times. Trailing 2-1 in the dying minutes of the game, Olimpia scored a dramatic last-gasp equalizer but, at the same time, a fan had creeped into the crowded box with a football of his own and dribbled toward goal and "scored" a second goal, seconds later. The Motagua players were furious but, unbelievably, the referee let the "first" Olimpia equalizer stand.

▼ Say Cheese!

http://y2u.be/yGwRKpZV4Ps

Players usually try to ignore pitch invaders, but Cristiano Ronaldo decided to buck the trend at Euro 2016 after Portugal's goalless draw with Austria. A young fan had somehow managed to slip past the stewards after the full-time whistle but, rather than call for security inside the Parc des Princes, the Real Madrid star agreed to pose for a selfie with the star-struck interloper. Ronaldo's generous gesture was even more admirable given that he'd missed a penalty and had a goal disallowed in the game.

BIZARRE SENDING-OFFS

A two-footed tackle or an elbow to the face are common ways to see red in football, but these players found more inventive methods to ensure an early bath.

▼ Poultry Punishment

http://y2u.be/XMX_0xqBYT0

Argentinian footballers are an excitable lot, and Carlos Tevez proved the point in 2004 when he was playing for Boca Juniors. The striker scored against Boca's arch rivals, River Plate, and went absolutely mental, ripping off his shirt and rampaging across the pitch. He then decided to celebrate with a weird chicken dance, flapping his arms by his side as he sprinted about, but that was the last straw for the match official, who controversially reached into his pocket and produced a red card.

Hat-trick Fool

http://y2u.be/ONJuxugVRO8

Defender Medi Dresevic was pretty pleased with himself when he scored a cracking goal to complete an unlikely hat-trick for his club, Norrby IF, in a Swedish third-division match in 2016. In fact, he was so excited that he sprinted off the pitch, jumped a security fence and sat in an empty stand, applauding himself. The smile was wiped well and truly off his face, however, when he rejoined his teammates, as the referee punished him for his antics with a second yellow card, and he was ordered off.

COCK-A-DOODLE-DON'T!

Ivorian Indecency

http://y2u.be/EReWfVzzsoE

It's hard to keep calm when you score a late equalizer, and Ivory Coast forward Dally Gbale definitely lost his cool when he was on target for his team, Freamunde, in a Portuguese second-tier league game against Chaves in 2014. The striker just couldn't contain himself and ran over to the Chaves fans, dropped his shorts and brandished his naked rear at them. The referee was having none of that and, after Gbale had covered himself up, he was promptly sent off.

Injustice for Inkoom

http://y2u.be/7MBcIJDa3ts

Ghanaian international Samuel Inkoom was already on his way off the pitch when he bizarrely saw red in a Ukrainian league match between his side, FC Dnipro, and Karpaty in 2011. The defender was in the process of being substituted but made the stupid mistake of taking his shirt off before he had reached the touchline, prompting the furious but picky referee to storm over and pointlessly show him a second yellow card, followed by a red one.

◄ Gun Crime

http://y2u.be/3L4w0qJJ5cA

Players who score from the penalty spot have plenty of time beforehand to plan their celebrations if they're on target, but PSG striker Edison Cavani probably should have given his some more thought in 2014. The Uruguayan made no mistake from 12 yards out against Lens and celebrated his score by kneeling down and making a rifle gesture toward the fans. Unsurprisingly, the referee was not amused at all and made it crystal clear it was time for Edison to have an early bath.

93

LUCKY GOALS

Some scores are the result of supreme skill, brilliant vision and outstanding team work, while some goals are no more than pure, outrageous luck.

▶ Fallen Hero

http://y2u.be/wFSfmLTv42I

There's no doubt Philipp Schobesberger should have scored for Rapid Vienna in their league game against Viktoria Plzen in 2015, but the way he eventually put the ball in the net definitely wasn't what he had planned. Put clean through by a teammate, the Austrian midfielder was about to shoot with his right foot but inexplicably lost his balance at the crucial moment and, as he hit the deck, somehow managed to accidentally poke the ball home with his left foot.

Wrong Foot

http://y2u.be/0NQjg5d_I5c

Senegal striker Papiss Cisse has scored goals for seven different clubs in his professional career, but none of his efforts were as fortunate as his hilarious effort for Shandong Luneng against Shanghai in China in 2016. The forward attempted a left-footed shot on the edge of the six-yard box but completely missed the ball. He also lost balance and, as both legs spun in the air, the striker inadvertently made contact with his right boot, lifting the ball over the keeper and into the goal.

Incredible Throw-in

http://y2u.be/a8EGgkXFUVA

A lucky – but also spectacular – effort, Randy Gordon's goal for the Hackensack Comets side over in the USA in 2013 was an unbelievable screamer. Gordon stunned the crowd when he did an athletic somersault in the process of taking a throw-in, but they were even more surprised when the ball flew high through the air, into the penalty area and, finally, over the shocked opposition goalkeeper for one of the unlikeliest goals you'll ever see.

A (LUCKY) NOSE FOR GOAL

▲ Wonderful Wood

http://y2u.be/AlWZdBsUYJA

Good strikers never stop chasing the ball, and persistence bizarrely paid dividends for Leicester City forward Chris Wood in 2014 with a goal against Watford he knew absolutely nothing about. There seemed no danger when the Hornets passed the ball back to keeper Manuel Almunia, but Wood kept running regardless and the Spanish stopper blasted his left-footed clearance smack into the forward's face, the ball ricocheting off the Leicester man into the back of the net.

IN THE DRESSING ROOM

The inner sanctum of every football team, the dressing room is also the setting for some of football's funniest comedy moments.

WON'T SOMEBODY THINK OF THE CLEANERS?

▲ Gunners' Joy

http://y2u.be/BaRj4dnBbOI

Winning the FA Cup is, of course, cause for celebration and the Arsenal team obviously agreed after their 2017 triumph over Chelsea at Wembley, judging by this dressing-room footage. Striker Alexis Sanchez is the man responsible for filming the clip, which reveals the Gunners having quite the party, with some dubious singing and very dodgy dancing inside the stadium. The bizarre moves in particular busted out by Egyptian midfielder Mohamed Elneny have to be seen to be believed.

THE WRONG
WAY TO USE
YOUR HEAD

▶ Dressing-room Dance Floor

http://y2u.be/cuJ5tSush7U

The Brazilian national team are known worldwide as the "Samba Kings", and their players definitely have rhythm, judging by this behind-the-scenes footage from 2017 of some of the side dancing in the dressing room. Featuring stars Neymar, Marcelo, Dani Alves, Marquinhos and Paulinho, the brilliant clip shows the five South Americans suddenly jump up and burst into a weird but oddly enjoyable routine that could perhaps be best compared to a group of hyperactive chickens at a disco.

◀ Temper, Temper!

http://y2u.be/yUsf30FuS9M

Footballers really hate getting sent off, and Polish striker Lukasz Teodorczyk was certainly fuming after he was shown a red card for diving in the penalty area while playing for Anderlecht in 2017. The look on the forward's face told a story but, if the fans thought he might calm down in the dressing room, they were very wrong, as cameras caught Teodorczyk storming down the tunnel and then headbutting the nearest door in frustration at his early bath.

FIVE-DIGIT CHEATS

Handballs are always controversial and, although eagle-eyed referees often spot the crime, sometimes players get away with it scot-free.

No Angel

http://y2u.be/4Rk66q0yqqM

A quickly taken throw-in can be a dangerous ploy, but you really have to wait for the ball to go out of play before you try it. Step forward Man United's Angel di Maria against Liverpool in 2015, who was so impatient to restart the game that he didn't bother with the ball going beyond the touchline, instead catching it on the pitch right in front of Liverpool boss Brendan Rodgers. The Reds gaffer went mental, while di Maria tried and failed to keep a straight face.

THE DADDY OF ALL HANDBALLS

▶ The Hand of God

http://y2u.be/-ccNkksrfls

The daddy of all handballs, Diego Maradona's infamous piece of skulduggery during the World Cup quarter-final between Argentina and England in Mexico in 1986 remains one of the tournament's biggest scandals. Exactly how referee Ali Bin Nasser could believe El Diego (five-foot five) was able to outjump Three Lions keeper Peter Shilton (six-foot one, plus his outstretched arms) remains a mystery, but the upshot was that the goal stood and England crashed out of the competition.

▼ Horrid Henry

http://y2u.be/l7slrw1fwA8

The legendary luck of the Irish deserted the Republic of Ireland team in 2009 when they were the victims to an inexcusable bit of cheating from Thierry Henry in their World Cup qualifying play-off game in Paris. With the second leg deadlocked 1-1 on aggregate and the game in extra-time, Henry twice used his hands in the Irish area to keep the ball in play and then shamelessly set up William Gallas for the winning header. Henry later confessed to his crime but FIFA were deaf to Ireland's pleas for a replay and the French sheepishly headed off to the World Cup.

THIERRY'S TRICKERY WENT UNPUNISHED

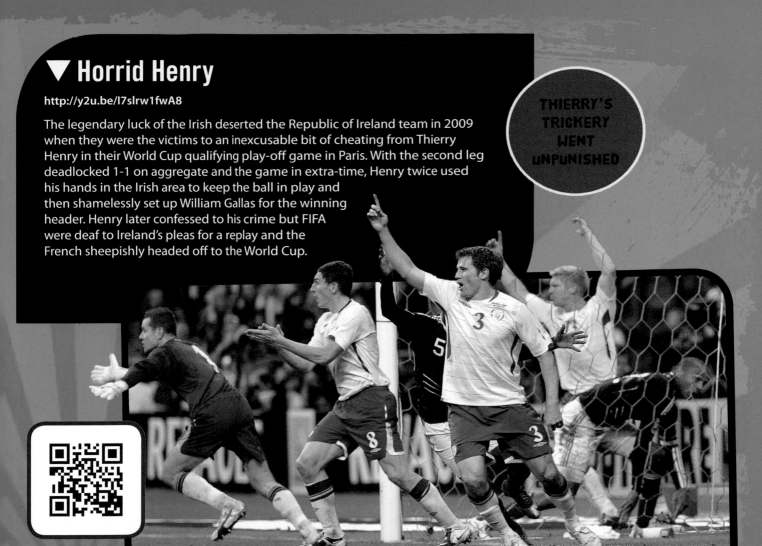

◀ What a Catch

http://y2u.be/wuteWxc7B78

Some handballs are subtle, while some are blatant. And then there's the strange case of the clash between Australia and Equatorial Guinea at the 2011 Women's World Cup, when Guinea defender Bruna caught the ball in her own penalty area for no apparent reason. The Aussies screamed for a penalty, but the referee just stood and watched as Bruna realized her mistake, casually dropped the ball and played on as if absolutely nothing had happened. Justice, however, was served, with Australia eventually running out 3-2 winners.

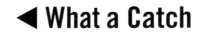

MASCOT MAYHEM

You don't have to be mad to dress up in an oversized comedy costume to entertain a football crowd, but it certainly helps.

▶ Monkey Madness

http://y2u.be/nRLeSbYjzfQ

Hartlepool United's mascot is a monkey called H'Angus who became so popular that he was actually voted in as the town's mayor! H'Angus – aka Stuart Drummond, the man inside the suit – got in a bit of bother in the early 2000s, when he was ejected from a couple of games for making rude gestures and smuggling in an inflatable doll but, in 2002, he decided to stand for election, promising free bananas for all school children. Unbelievably, he won and, for the next 11 years, Hartlepool's mayor was a monkey.

Fishy Fun

http://y2u.be/tJ8p4DD2DhM

Half-time of Derby County's league showdown with Blackburn Rovers in 2016 was one of the weirdest cases ever of mascot mayhem, which ended in one of the Derby staff getting eaten. The greedy mascot was a fish called "Mackerel Jordan", who attacked the County goalkeeping coach and then completely consumed the poor bloke in its giant mouth, gobbling him down, head first. Thankfully, the fella re-emerged a minute later, now only wearing his boxer shorts and football socks, and made a comedy run for it.

ON THE CAMPAIGN TRAIL

▶ Touchline Terror

http://y2u.be/SaNhCbAaWQQ

Some mascots are cute, cuddly and child friendly, but that couldn't be said for Partick Thistle's Kingsley. A terrifying, spiky yellow creature, the Thistle mascot is enough to give kids nightmares and was unleashed on an unsuspecting public for the first time in 2015. Pictures of Kingsley were soon doing the rounds on social media, and most people were seriously unimpressed with the club's bizarre creation. "Were I a child," tweeted one stunned supporter, "this would make me wet my pants."

◀ Wolf Attack

http://y2u.be/Ez0gd78zkJk

In the famous children's story, the Big Bad Wolf and the Three Little Pigs weren't the best of friends, and it was the same story in 1998 when Wolverhampton Wanderers travelled to Ashton Gate to play Bristol City. Wolves mascot, "Wolfie", tried to borrow a ball from the pigs, but they weren't in the mood to share and a fight broke out. The scrapping mascots were eventually thrown out of the stadium but "Wolfie" obviously liked the attention and, the following week, ran out on the pitch to the Rocky theme tune.

THE STUFF OF NIGHTMARES

THE SILVER SCREEN

Players are constantly being accused of play acting when they take a dive, and these footballers obviously decided to try and make the most of their theatrical talents.

◀ Cowboy Cinema

http://y2u.be/JMd6YNUk9nQ

Paul Breitner won the World Cup with West Germany in 1974, but the former Bayern Munich and Real Madrid defender really hit the heights when he appeared in a spaghetti western called *Potato Fritz* two years later. Breitner played a character called Sergeant Stark in the film about a group of German soldiers in the old American Wild West but, despite his best efforts, the acting career never took off and he went back to the day job.

▶ Looking for Eric

http://y2u.be/UaRi-79yRw4

As a player, Eric Cantona used to "ghost" into the penalty box on a regular basis for Man United and France, and the striker was able to use his skill once again as an actor when he appeared in the 2009 film *Looking for Eric*. Playing a ghostly version of himself, Cantona appears to a football-loving, down-on-his-luck postman who dispenses pearls of wisdom about life, family and fate but who, sadly, failed to reveal the secrets of the perfect free kick.

Neymar Acts Up

http://y2u.be/ZgJtc__K8sg

Playmaker Neymar is usually the star turn when he plays for club and country, but the Brazilian failed to steal the show when he made an awkward cameo in 2017 blockbuster *xXx: Return of Xander Cage*. Neymar's appearance began with a bizarre conversation in a café with Hollywood legend Samuel L. Jackson and climaxed with the player knocking out a shotgun-wielding bad guy with a metal napkin holder, which he kicks off a table. Unsurprisingly, he didn't get an Oscar nomination for his acting debut.

▲ Doctor in the House

http://y2u.be/q6XF66xysgQ

French defender Frank Leboeuf was a big name in English football when he played for Chelsea in the late 1990s, helping the Blues win a couple of FA Cups but, when he left Stamford Bridge and headed back to France, everyone quickly forgot about him. That was until 2014 when the Stephen Hawking biopic, *The Theory of Everything*, was released in cinemas and, suddenly, there was Leboeuf playing a Swiss doctor in one of the scenes.

▼ Wartime Adventures

http://y2u.be/abO0lm6L4T0

The daddy of all football flicks, *Escape To Victory*, was released in 1981 and tells the story of a group of prisoners in the Second World War who escape the clutches of the Germans after an exhibition match. Featuring greats of the game such as Brazil's Pele, England legend Bobby Moore and Ossie Ardiles of Argentina, the film also stars Sylvester Stallone, who, legend has it, was so useless at "playing" a footballer that the director decided to cast the Hollywood muscleman as the team's goalkeeper to avoid the embarrassment of watching him trying to kick a ball.

A STAR-STUDDED KICKABOUT

THE
DEFINITION
OF A SUPER
SUB

▶ Legendary Lewandowski

http://y2u.be/PWhDJ577AhQ

Polish striker Robert Lewandowski has made a habit of banging in goals for Bayern Munich over the years, but even he must have been surprised at his record-breaking haul against Wolfsburg in 2015. The forward bagged his first goal in the 51st minute, and went on to add four more in less than nine minutes. What's more, Lewandowski didn't even start the match! He'd come on at half time, setting the record for most goals scored by a substitute in the Bundesliga – one of four he set on the day.

GOALKEEPER GAFFES

Keepers can go from hero to zero in an instant. Here's the embarrassing proof there's nowhere to hide when careless custodians make costly blunders.

Terrible Taibi

http://y2u.be/esFAGx7RDL4

Italian stopper Massimo Taibi cost Man United £4.5 million back in 1999, but most agreed it was a complete waste of money after he produced one of the funniest gaffes in Premier League history. The Red Devils were playing Southampton at Old Trafford when the butter-fingered keeper allowed Matt Le Tissier's weak shot from 25 yards to go through his hands, under his body and finally between his legs for the softest goal imaginable. The following week he was part of the United side hammered 5-0 by Chelsea, and he never played for the club again.

▼ World Cup Clanger

http://y2u.be/9AWLpjhwu0c

There's never a good time to let in a horror goal, and England's Robert Green must surely have wished he didn't leave it until the 2010 World Cup to produce his own moment of madness. With England leading 1-0 against the USA, Green seemed to have Clint Dempsey's hopeful, long-range effort comfortably covered but, rather than cradle the weak shot into his chest like a new-born baby, the keeper let the ball slide off his gloves and roll apologetically into the net, gifting the Americans a shock 1-1 draw.

▶ Higuita's Horror Show

http://y2u.be/tT790tEixVA

Any goalkeeper who decides to have a dribble outside his area is definitely asking for trouble and that's exactly what Colombia's Rene Higuita got at the 1990 World Cup when he attempted an audacious Cruyff turn halfway up the pitch. Sadly for him, he was dispossessed by Cameroon's Roger Milla and the African striker then strolled casually toward the Colombia goal and, despite Higuita's desperate two-footed lunge, Milla slotted home for probably the easiest goal of his career.

Silly Sammy

http://y2u.be/feMkeG-SxkM

When it comes to unbelievable goalkeeper own goals, it's hard to beat Sammy Ndjock's effort playing for Minnesota United against Bournemouth in a pre-season friendly in 2016. There seemed no danger when Ndjock safely collected a punt forward, but he then wound up a long throw out, only to completely mess it up and accidentally hurl the ball toward his own net. The keeper desperately sprinted back to try and spare his blushes, but it was sadly too little too late.

▲ Not Very Safe Hans

http://y2u.be/9EqTaohqgL8

Bayer Leverkusen keeper Hans Jorg Butt was a very happy chap in 2004 when he scored from the penalty spot against Schalke. The only problem was that Butt was so excited by his score that he decided to celebrate with half his teammates on the way back to his goal and, while he was enjoying five minutes of fame, Schalke took a quick restart and Mike Hanke went for goal from the halfway line. Butt still hadn't got back, and the ball sailed into the unguarded net.

Two Left Feet

http://y2u.be/XiGC4GV0kHc

Plenty of keepers miss-kick bobbly back passes, but not many simply fall over for no apparent reason, collapse in a heap and allow the ball to roll between their legs and over the line. Step forward poor Virgil Vries, who earned himself Internet notoriety in 2011 for achieving that very feat when playing for South African side Golden Arrows against Amazulu. The embarrassed look on his face after his unexpected and costly tumble said it all.

GOAL OR NO GOAL?

Goal-line technology has finally arrived and it's here to stay. Judging by these curious "ghost goals", it's about time too.

▼ Crossbar Karma

http://y2u.be/o5QlBHF6ib8

Germany may have been on the wrong end of a crucial goal line ruling in the 1966 World Cup final at Wembley, but luck was finally on their side in the 2010 World Cup quarter-final against England, proving again that what goes around comes around. Leading 2-1 in Bloemfontein, the Germans thought they'd conceded an equalizer when Frank Lampard's shot hit the crossbar and landed a full two metres over the line, but this time the football gods were on their side and the referee said no goal. Germany won 4-1 and, from their point of view at least, justice was finally served.

▶ Slipping Through the Net

http://y2u.be/vQZmRqxnH6M

One of the game's strangest "goals" ever, Steffan Kiessling's bizarre header for Bayer Leverkusen against Hoffenheim in the German Bundesliga in 2013 was definitely a puzzler. Everything seemed perfectly normal as Kiessling rose highest to head home a corner, and both sets of players regrouped without protest for the restart. It was only later, thanks to the TV replays, that it became clear the ball had somehow past through the side netting of the goal and should never have been awarded.

▼ Late Arrival

http://y2u.be/x0hzqhTBIQo

Guilty goalkeepers are always desperate to make up for their mistakes, and Tottenham's Heurelho Gomes thought he'd done just that when he let Frank Lampard's soft, long shot slip through his fingers and between his legs when Tottenham played Chelsea in 2011. The Brazilian crawled back like a hyperactive toddler as the ball trickled lazily toward the goal, stopping the ball on the line, but his relief quickly turned to disbelief when the referee wrongly decided he'd got back too late to spare his blushes.

BEST TODDLER IMPRESSION

▶ Qualification Shocker

http://y2u.be/Txw1gPURFT0

In the big scheme of things, some ghost goals don't count for much, but others really do matter. Take Panama's goal against Costa Rica in 2017, a score awarded after a goal-mouth scramble during which the ball clearly never crossed the line. The referee, however, thought otherwise and blew his whistle, and Panama went on to win the game 2-1. The problem was that the lucky result meant Panama, rather than the USA, qualified for the 2018 World Cup finals, which, understandably, quite upset the Americans.

OUR FURRY FRIENDS

The beautiful game and the animal kingdom are not a great combination, as these strange cases of furry pitch invaders prove.

Brodie's Body Flow

http://y2u.be/ptt-gLTGhHE

Dogs are supposed to be a man's best friend, but there were definitely no thoughts of friendship on Chic Brodie's mind back in 1970 after the Brentford goalkeeper ran into a stray sheepdog on the pitch during a game against Colchester United. It might have been funny, but Brodie actually shattered his kneecap in the canine collision, and the injury brought his career to a premature end. "The dog might have been a small one," Brodie said, "but it just happened to be a solid one."

THIS PITCH INVADER JUST WOULDN'T MOO-VE

▼ Bovine Bother

http://y2u.be/zAeALo0cSyA

Most animal pitch invaders tend to be on the small size, but it was a massive lump of a beast that interrupted a friendly between Bulgarian side Botev Plovdiv and AEL Limassol from Cyprus in 2017. The gatecrasher was a huge cow, which had got through a broken wire fence around the ground and proceeded to wander around the pitch as if it owned it. The players had no choice but to let the cow take its time before it finally ambled away so the game could begin.

◀ Marauding Moggy

http://y2u.be/Vfc_PF9V5ks

If cats really do have nine lives, the frisky feline that interrupted proceedings during Liverpool's Premier League clash with Spurs in 2012 probably used up at least one of them after it scampered onto the Anfield pitch in front of 40,000 fans. A steward eventually managed to catch the confused moggy and it was later renamed Shankly, after Liverpool's legendary manager, Bill Shankly. The stray cat proved so popular that, within hours of its pitch invasion, its spoof Twitter account had more than 30,000 followers.

SPURS' LATEST SIGNING

▶ When Animals Attack!

http://y2u.be/45FoC7PqyJc

Pine martins have a reputation as fierce predators and this was painfully obvious when one of the furry critters invaded the pitch during the FC Thun and BSC Young Boys Swiss league clash in 2013. The animal successfully evaded capture for a few minutes, bringing the game to a temporary halt but, when Young Boys player Loris Benito finally managed to grab the uninvited guest, the martin sunk its teeth into his hand. To be fair to Benito, he clung on to his attacker despite the injury, and the game carried on.

THE MUSIC MEN

Lots of people dream of becoming a pop star, and footballers are no different, but these players foolishly tried to make their dreams come true.

▶ Big Bad Vinnie

http://y2u.be/7Nz5F2aIWzw

Midfield-hardman-turned-Hollywood-star Vinnie Jones has enjoyed great success in his post-football career as an actor, but the same couldn't be said of his foray into pop. The former Wimbledon and Wales player appeared on the BBC's *Top of the Pops* in 2002 to perform his cover version of 1970s classic "Big Bad Leroy Brown", but his performance failed to wow the viewers and Jones wisely decided acting, rather than singing, was his best bet.

◀ I Can't Dance

http://y2u.be/RhmJFOa4RgQ

These days, Holland legend Ruud Gullit sports a very sensible short haircut when he's doing his TV punditry but, back in his playing days, he was famous for his flowing dreadlocks. It was, then, probably inevitable that his first attempt at being a pop star would be with a reggae track. Gullit's tune "Not the Dancing Kind" was released in 1984 and was a modest hit, but Bob Marley it was not.

▼ Bonkers Ballad

http://y2u.be/3MnMskejuvc

It's fair to say that 1979 was a good year for Kevin Keegan. The England striker won the Bundesliga title with Hamburg and he was voted European Footballer of the Year, so it really was a shame that he had to undo all his good work by releasing his awful single "Head Over Heels in Love". A toe-curling ballad that saw KK warbling away in the biggest flares in the history of fashion and an enormous shirt collar, the tune – amazingly – hung around the charts for six full weeks. Which absolutely no one was head over heels about.

New Order Up

http://y2u.be/Re4aDJL3heA

The World Cup song is a grand English tradition, and few efforts have been as successful as New Order's "World In Motion". The track shot to the top of the UK Singles Chart ahead of the 1990 FIFA World Cup in Italy, and featured backing vocals from several members of the England team, but the breakout star was none other than England winger John Barnes. The former Liverpool player demonstrated his rapping skills, in a guest verse, though its fair to say that his lyrical talents didn't quite match up to those on the pitch.

▼ Misleading Title

http://y2u.be/M9UHcRrCWll

Back in 1999, Andy Cole was at the peak of his footballing powers, banging in the goals for Manchester United and lifting the Champions League trophy, and it probably seemed the perfect time for the England striker to have a dabble in the music business. Cue the release of his R'n'B single "Outstanding" but, sadly for the United star, his effort proved to be anything but outstanding and, after reaching a lowly number 68 in the charts in its first week on sale, the single sunk without a trace, and Cole went back to kicking a ball about for a living.

THE NUMBER TWOS

Assistant managers usually avoid the spotlight, but occasionally they find themselves unavoidably as the centre of attention.

A VERY ANGRY ASSISTANT

◀ Naughty McPhee

http://y2u.be/JK3QFj8mD1o

Hearts assistant boss Austin McPhee found himself in the headlines for the wrong reasons in 2017 during his side's SPL showdown with Hamilton. Standing on the edge of the technical area, McPhee stopped Hamilton's Darian MacKinnon taking a quick throw-in and, as the pair grappled for the ball, they both took a tumble. The incident sparked an ugly dugout scuffle, and it was only brought to an end when the Hearts Number Two was ordered to the stands by the referee.

▶ Hammers Tumble

http://y2u.be/ZmlcmdEUvzk

All eyes are usually on the manager in the dugout as he barks out his orders, but West Ham Number Two Neil McDonald accidently stole the limelight at Upton Park in 2012 when gravity suddenly got the better of him. McDonald was waving his arms about excitedly behind boss Sam Allardyce but should have focused on his feet, as he slipped on the greasy turf, did the splits and then fell, crashing backward into the dugout with his legs in the air.

◄ Pisa Slap

http://y2u.be/C1FKiUxTGlc

If you were being polite, you'd call former Italy midfielder Gennaro Gattuso a fiery character. If you weren't being so tactful, you'd describe him as an absolute nutter, and he definitely lost the plot in 2016 when he was the manager of Pisa. Gattuso was unhappy with something he saw out on the pitch but, rather than scream at his players, he turned around and gave his poor Number Two a slap across the face for no good reason at all.

Walk of Shame

http://y2u.be/JKPcVaFUaUM

It's not unusual for unruly coaching staff to be told to get out of the dugout by referees. Banishment to the dressing room is one of the punishments in such circumstances, but this proved difficult for the Celta Vigo Number Two in 2017 when he was told to make himself scarce. His problem was that the dugout was on the opposite side of the pitch to the tunnel, meaning he had to take an embarrassing and lonely walk across the pitch in front of the whole stadium.

THAT'S GATTUSO'S SECRET: HE'S ALWAYS ANGRY

Oscar for Acevedo

http://y2u.be/MoFNem6RzKE

Coaching staff really should set a good example to their players but, sadly, the assistant manager of Uruguayan side Defensor Sporting did the complete opposite in 2017. Alejandro Acevedo stormed onto the pitch to protest with the referee but was shown a red card for his troubles and one of the linesmen had to come between them. Acevedo then tried to con the referee into thinking his assistant had headbutted him, flinging himself to the ground in hilarious and theatrical fashion, even though there had been absolutely no crime committed.

115

PHYSIO FAILS

Injured players rely on the expert help of physios and team doctors, but sometimes medical staff make the headlines for all the wrong reasons.

▼ Lewin's Leap

http://y2u.be/7UaQxt1OUP4

England's woeful World Cup campaign in Brazil in 2014 was one to try to forget and, arguably, the most lasting memory was created when physio Gary Lewin was stretchered off during the Three Lions' group game against Italy. Lewin leaped up in celebration in the dugout when Daniel Sturridge scored for England in the first half, but he landed on a water bottle on the way down and dislocated his ankle, forcing medical colleagues to call for the stretcher and rush him to the nearest hospital.

WHEN CELEBRATIONS GO WRONG

▶ DIY Solution

http://y2u.be/ZtBvvnIYKf0

Electric buggies carrying off injured players are a common sight at matches these days, but lower-league football can't always afford such expensive medical transport. The Romanian fourth-division clash between Timisul Urseni and SS Politehnica in 2013 was a case in point, but one of the physios came up with a cunning plan and, when one of the players went down, he comically came out onto the pitch riding a motorized wheelbarrow and then drove the crocked footballers off in his bizarre homemade contraption.

Pompey Pile-up

http://y2u.be/69kpMBSirlE

Getting onto the pitch as quickly as possible to treat an injured player is a part of the physio's job description, and the two medical chaps at Portsmouth's Fratton Park ground in 2010 were certainly going at full speed as they raced out to assess their patients. Hilariously, however, they weren't paying enough attention to each other and, as their paths crossed, the visiting physio ran right behind his Portsmouth counterpart, accidentally clipped his heels and spectacularly sent him flying.

Emergency Keeper

http://y2u.be/afhWQumYO24

Brazilian football has produced some great comedy moments over the years, and this one from a play-off game between Aparecidence and Tupi in 2013 was an absolute cracker. Tupi were on the attack and looked to have found a way through the defence, only for the over-excited Aparecidence physio, who was lurking near the goal, to clear Tupi's first shot off the line, with the goalkeeper beaten, and then make a second "save" with his legs. Unsurprisingly, the angry Tupi players then chased the mental medical man off the pitch.

Mental Medic

http://y2u.be/qzvmy8uMXPU

There were crazy scenes in Colombia in 2013 when Cobreloa welcomed La Equidad, and the visiting physio got rather too hot under the collar. Cobreloa striker Miguel Angel Cuellar fouled the goalkeeper in the area and got embroiled in a scuffle with the stopper's angry teammates, but he really should have been keeping an eye on the La Equidad physio, who came sprinting along the touchline at speed and launched a flying headbutt on the unsuspecting forward.

SKILLS SHOWCASE

A spectacular trick is guaranteed to get the crowd on their feet, and these examples of sublime skill are five of the best ever.

▶ Breaking the Rules

http://y2u.be/hQ-uwzo27S4

Most goalkeepers don't enjoy taking unnecessary risks outside their area, but former Manchester United stopper Fabien Barthez wasn't one of them and, back at Old Trafford in 2001, he lived the dream when he outrageously nutmegged an outfield player. The unlucky chap was Derby County's Lee Morris, who was left looking very foolish indeed as the Frenchman rolled the ball between his legs when he really should have done the decent thing and smashed it up field.

◀ Wazza's Wager

http://y2u.be/hql4zZ_ktNw

When Nike were filming a TV advert in 2009, the star of the show was meant to be Wayne Rooney, but it was actually a 19-year-old by the name of Callam Roberts who grabbed the glory in front of the cameras. The teenager bet the England star he could nutmeg him during a five-a-side game and Rooney accepted the wager. Cue Roberts successfully slipping the ball through the striker's legs and, in the process, winning himself a couple of tickets for Man United's next home game.

The Flying Flick

http://y2u.be/AiubgXwPB_8

The volley has always been one of the beautiful game's toughest skills to master, but it's even more difficult when you try to hit one with a flying back heel. Many have tried and failed to execute this outrageous trick but Metalist Kharkiv midfielder Cleiton Xavier pulled it off spectacularly in a game against Dnipro in 2011, flicking a cross into the back of the net with a stunning mid-air touch from behind his back.

▼ "The Blanco"

http://y2u.be/_G237cypBq8

Football's answer to the kangaroo, maverick Mexican winger Cuauhtemoc Blanco, lit up the 1998 World Cup finals in France with an ingenious move called – you've guessed it – "The Blanco". Faced by two South Korean players, the cheeky wide man wedged the ball between his feet and then jumped between the pair of opponents, releasing the ball just before hitting the ground and sprinting clear of the two confused defenders.

▼ Thierry's Trick

http://y2u.be/OhR-WnafzoE

Houdini was famous for his ability to escape from seemingly impossible situations, but the great showman could still probably have learned a thing or two from Arsenal striker Thierry Henry. The Frenchman's brilliant bit of skill came in 2004 when he stole the ball from Middlesbrough's Danny Mills by the corner flag, and then got out of the tightest of situations with a ridiculous nutmeg, dancing past the red-faced defender, who probably thought he had the silky Frenchman safely trapped in the corner.

HAIRY HORRORS

Football has enjoyed more than its fair share of dodgy haircuts and dubious styles, as these eye-watering examples certainly prove.

◄ Ready and Abel

http://y2u.be/hcl9XajSULo

A man who had almost as many outlandish haircuts during his professional career as the games he played, Abel Xavier (or Abel Luís da Silva Costa Xavier if we're going to be formal) was a true "Renaissance Man" when it came to styling and facial hair. Perhaps his most eye-catching creation was a daring combination of thick corn rows on top (bleached blonde, obviously), with a classic goatee (also blonde) to set it all off. Subtle it wasn't.

► Crazy Colombian

http://y2u.be/zp7vf5So3_k

Carlos Valderrama's hair was so big that he could have stashed a spare pair of shin pads and a water bottle in there, and no one would have been any the wiser. The legendary Colombian midfielder just loved his blonde, tight, corkscrew-perm look and, as he ran across the pitch, his hair seemed to take on a life all of its own. Suggestions that he was actually wearing an elaborate wig were never confirmed by the man himself.

THE HAIR TO MATCH THE SHIRT

▶ Green and Mean

http://y2u.be/fTuBBw_wJ5g

Standing at over six feet tall, it was difficult to miss Taribo West during a match, but the big Nigerian made absolutely sure he wasn't overlooked by sporting one of the game's most unforgettable hairstyles of all time. Shaving most of his head, dying his remaining locks green and then gelling them up for a must-have antenna-style look, the defender looked like something from a low-rent sci-fi film – although no one was ever brave or stupid enough to tell him.

◀ Wonder of Waddle

http://y2u.be/xZTmcDpRDgo

Pop star, mercurial winger, natural entertainer and the owner of arguably football's worst ever mullet, Chris Waddle was a man of many talents – and a terrible, terrible hairstyle. The England star made no apologies for his heinous crime against fashion and, as his mullet got longer and longer, the sniggers from the terraces grew louder and louder.

AN 80S ICON... AND CHRIS WADDLE

A Team to Dye For

http://y2u.be/ii3ja39mkM4

Individual innovation in the hair stakes is all well and good, but the Romanian team raised the bar during the 1998 World Cup when they decided, en masse, to bleach their hair ahead of their group game with Tunisia. The collective coiffuring was to celebrate qualifying for the knockout stages, and the side emerged from the tunnel at the Stade de France in Paris with blond bonces to a man, presenting the bemused match commentators with one of the toughest 90 minutes of their careers.

FOOTBALL IN THE STICKS

The professional game has the glitz and the glamour, but grass-roots football still produces its fair share of quirky tales and bizarre stories

Madron Massacred

http://y2u.be/wb2lyHnj46E

Enjoyment is the name of the game when it comes to village football, but it's a safe bet that the hapless players of Cornish side Madron didn't enjoy themselves in 2010 when they found themselves on the wrong end of an eye-watering 55-0 scoreline against Illogan. The fact that it was actually against the Illogan reserve team only rubbed salt into the wound, but Madron didn't do themselves any favours when they turned up for the game with just seven players. "I know everybody is probably laughing at us," admitted club secretary Alan Davenport after the team's nightmare 90 minutes.

▼ Outrageous OAP

http://y2u.be/41hX9Mlcfkg

Many village clubs have produced their own calendars in a bid to boost their coffers, but none of them were surely as eye-catching as Ancaster Athletic's 2008 effort, which featured a naked appearance from 102-year-old Nora Hardwick. "Miss November" decided to strip off after living in the Lincolnshire village for more than 70 years but insisted her contribution was as "artistic" as possible. "It was all very tastefully done," Nora said. "You couldn't see any of the bits or anything."

ANCASTER'S CALENDAR GIRL

A WET AND WILD CONTEST

▲ Water on the Pitch

http://y2u.be/MaMEHdyKXR4

The right choice of footwear for a match can be critical and, for players of the Bourton-on-the-Water team in the Cotswolds, it probably should be wellingtons rather than football boots. That's because, for the past 70 odd years, Bourton have played their home games on the Windrush River in the village, rather than on a traditional grass-covered surface, with the goals set up under two bridges that span the three-metre wide stream. Thankfully, the water is only knee high, meaning players are in more danger of getting booked for diving than they are of drowning.

The Italian Job

http://y2u.be/QLLMz1jhhS0

Village sides rarely enjoy the luxury of playing abroad, but West Auckland were the exception to the rule back in 1909 when they unexpectedly found themselves playing the mighty Juventus in Italy. The County Durham team were invited to Turin to compete in the inaugural Sir Thomas Lipton trophy because the English Football Association had refused to send an XI and, against all the odds, the West Auckland side, made up of amateurs and miners, thrashed Juventus 6-1 in the final.

What's in a Name?

http://y2u.be/ktoOGZ57Lg4

It's not unusual for a couple of players in the same team to share a surname, even if they're not related, but the name game got seriously out of hand in 2012 at Bungay FC in Suffolk when all 22 players on show (not to mention the referee, linesmen, substitutes and even the mascot) were called Bungay. The bizarre game was the brainchild of club official Shaun Cole, who invited Bungays from Britain, as well as from America and Australia, to take part in the charity match, which made a mockery of the referee writing down anyone's name in his book.

TOUCHLINE JITTERS

You don't have to have a sense of humour to be an assistant referee but, judging by these comical mishaps, it certainly helps.

Avian Attack

http://y2u.be/RKFNJWcHycA

Assistant match officials usually have more than enough on their plate dealing with angry players, mental managers and thousands of screaming supporters who are furious with their last offside call. Linesman Maycon Vieira, however, had another touchline headache during a Brazilian league match in 2013, when he was repeatedly dive bombed by an angry bird. The flying attacker just wouldn't leave poor Vieira alone, and he was repeatedly forced to duck out of the way of its aerial assault.

▼ The Circle Line

http://y2u.be/OVkf2owHNGA

The introduction of vanishing spray has given football some great comedy moments, and one of the best was on show in 2012 in Brazil when Corinthians faced Santos. A free kick was awarded to Santos near the touchline, and the linesman stepped forward with his aerosol to mark out where he wanted the Corinthian players to stand. They tried to steal a few cheeky yards by standing to the side of his straight line, so the assistant referee marched back on and hilariously sprayed a giant, 10-metre semicircle so there was absolutely no doubt.

▼ Water Hazard

http://y2u.be/L3cr2fFOrJc

It's important for footballers to stay well hydrated. It's why many touchlines are littered with water bottles, in readiness for players to take a quick slip, but these drinks represent a real hazard to unsuspecting linesman. Step forward the unfortunate assistant referee who was running the line in DC United's game against Tauro in the USA in 2014, only to be embarrassingly felled by a stray bottle that he failed to spot.

The Fallen Flag

http://y2u.be/2zhxalZFeA0

The first lesson assistant referees learn at linesman school is to look after their flags. It is their most important bit of kit and, without it, they'd be out of a job. The linesman for Portugal's international with Serbia in 2015 didn't seem to know this and, as he strolled casually along the touchline, he was left red-faced when his flag slowly slipped off its pole. Emergency repairs were required but not before his mishap was caught on camera.

▶ An Early Bath

http://y2u.be/D5S3FbP589k

Linesmen are used to getting verbal abuse from fans. Running up and down the touchline makes them an easy target for the terraces but Partizan Belgrade supporters took it to another level in 2015. The helpless assistant referee probably thought he was safe, given the row of security guards between him and the crowd, but they were powerless to stop him getting soaked with a bucketful of what looked like extremely cold water. To add insult to injury, they then chucked the bucket at him.

REFRESHING OR DEPRESSING?

▼ Wet and Wild

http://y2u.be/rGDzCgnx-50

Playing football in the rain is nothing new, but the deluge that struck the 2017 Africa Cup of Nations game between Mali and Uganda was almost biblical in proportion. A downpour immediately before the match left puddles dotting the pitch, with both sets of players gamely trying to compete in comical conditions. Unsurprisingly, chances were few and far between. The soggy contest ended in a 0-0 draw, a result that sent both teams crashing out of the tournament.

MAKING A SPLASH AT AFCON

DIDN'T SEE THAT COMING!

Not all footballers are famed for their brain power, but these ingenious goals show there are some players with plenty going on upstairs

▶ Cunning Coventry

http://y2u.be/_FxSKczJprl

Englishman Ernie Hunt scored more than 150 goals during his career but none better than his ingenious stunner for Coventry against Everton during the 1970–71 season. The Sky Blues were awarded a free kick outside the area and midfielder Willie Carr stood over the ball. What happened next took everyone's breath away: Carr cleverly flicked the ball into the air behind his back and Hunt was on hand to unleash an unstoppable right-footed volley, which rocketed into the top corner of the Everton goal.

Free-kick Farce

http://y2u.be/60CD4OWnljk

The Borussia Dortmund "B" side came up with an imaginative free-kick routine in 2013 that had their opponents completely fooled. Six Dortmund players gathered around the ball to discuss their plan but, when it came to actually executing their routine, it looked like they'd made a mess of it. The mistake, however, was merely a ploy and, as everyone stood around looking lost, Konstantin Fring popped up and scored with a beautiful curling left-footed effort past the static goalkeeper.

Rearly Good

http://y2u.be/EONwFzetSTM

Footballers have make to split-second decisions during a match, and Czech defender David Hovorka was certainly thinking clearly in action for the Sparta Prague second team in 2013. Attacking a cross in the opposition box, Hovorka rapidly realized he wasn't going to be able to touch either his head or a boot to the ball, so he improvised, turning in mid-air to make contact with his bum. Remarkably, his unusual tactic worked and the ball trickled into the back of the net.

Inventive Ishibitsu

http://y2u.be/7NDc_UtYs2Q

Confusing the opposition is the key to an effective free-kick routine, and it's safe to say Kyoto Sanga's opponents in Japan were completely baffled after watching their bizarre manoeuvre in 2014. Five Kyoto players lined up behind the ball but the first four were all decoys, each of them, in turn, faking a shot before getting out of the way. It was left to defender Yosuke Ishibitsu to actually hit it, his top-corner thunderbolt giving the keeper absolutely no chance.

▼ Corner Confusion

http://y2u.be/KzBAyW15Ocl

The New York Red Bulls had obviously been reading the rules of the game, judging by the ingenious goal they scored against Chicago Fire in 2015. Awarded a corner, the Bulls' Lloyd Sam, went over and tapped the ball but then strolled away and left it to Sacha Kljestan. What Chicago didn't spot was that Sam had actually already taken the corner, meaning Kljestan could legally dribble into the box and, in the chaos and confusion that followed, New York scored through Ronald Zubar.

A SNEAKY SET PIECE

CUNNING GOALS

Scoring goals is sometimes all about brain over brawn and, as these clever scores prove, it can pay to use your head when you're on the pitch.

▶ Drinks Break

http://y2u.be/rRJUAZxnnOw

Brazilian playmaker Ronaldinho had magic in his boots, and the goal he created for his side, Atlético Mineiro, in 2013 was pure genius. Mineiro were awarded a throw-in, but there was a break in play and Ronaldinho went for a drink and a quick chat with the Sao Paulo keeper in the area. The defence paid him no attention but, when play restarted, Ronaldinho was all alone in the box, picking up possession from the throw before setting up a tap-in for a teammate.

Step-over Stars

http://y2u.be/Y0r_nAzFP78

This brilliant goal was definitely a team effort and was scored by the Serbian U-17 side in a match against their Moldovan counterparts in 2012. Serbia were awarded a corner, which was drilled low to the edge of the box. Three Serbian players in succession failed to pick up possession, but all three actually stepped over the ball and, with the Moldova defence by now totally confused, there was winger Andrija Zivkovic with all the time and space he could wish for to pick his spot and score.

▶ Back Pass

http://y2u.be/bfO3hBttoQQ

The 1998 clash between Sheffield United and Port Vale produced one of the smartest goals ever seen and it was all down to the quick thinking of Blades striker Dean Saunders. Chasing a long punt forward, Saunders was beaten to the ball by the Vale keeper, who conceded a throw-in. No United players were up in support, so Saunders grabbed the ball, threw it against the back of the retreating stopper and hit a brilliant first-time shot, which went into the unguarded goal.

NEVER TURN YOUR BACK

▼ Spot Kick One-two

http://y2u.be/ocvPaBxa4Xc

Lionel Messi is deadly from the penalty spot but the Barcelona superstar decided to share the love in 2016 with an inventive ploy that had Celta Vigo's players scratching their heads. Nothing seemed out of the ordinary when the Argentinian placed the ball on the spot and ran in but, rather than swing his trusty left boot and shooting, he laid it off with a cheeky pass to teammate Luis Suarez, who had the simple job of side-footing past the confused Celta keeper.

Fight Club

http://y2u.be/cFavq7mhvxA

Teams put hours of practice into their free-kick routines on the training ground, but few have ever come up with a tactic as ingenious as the one used by Israeli side Hapoel Ra'anana in 2012. Setting up their set piece just outside of the box, two Hapoel players appeared to fall about and began to push each other. With all eyes on the feuding pair, striker Avo Knafo was on hand to quietly step up and curl the ball into the back of the net.

LOSING THE PLOT

Football players are of course competitive by nature, but sometimes the will to win can suddenly explode into acts of pure insanity.

Evil Elizabeth

http://y2u.be/pJLSUpVoZt8

If you're a downright dirty defender, the sight of a ponytailed striker is probably just too much to resist, and University of Mexico defender Elizabeth Lambert proved the point during a Mountain West Conference semi-final in 2009 when she got a glimpse of the opposition striker. Not content with yanking the poor forward's hair when the referee wasn't looking, naughty Lambert also landed a vicious short-armed punch into her victim's back. Justice was served, however, when she received a two-match ban after officials reviewed the video evidence.

▶ ZZ Over the Top

http://y2u.be/TwQnQeGdsUY

Perhaps the most infamous (and stupidly acquired) red card in football history, Zinedine Zidane's headbutt in the 2006 World Cup final between France and Italy was pure madness. The ball was nowhere near the French playmaker when he decided to attack Marco Materazzi, leaving the Azzurri defender in a heap on the grass. Unluckily for Zidane, both the referee and the cameras saw his stupid assault and, as he headed for an early bath, France were beaten by the Italians in a penalty shootout.

▼ Kung Fu Fighting

http://y2u.be/wo2aUfwPQvs

No player likes getting sent off, and Man United legend Eric Cantona definitely wasn't happy when he saw red against Crystal Palace in 1995. His mood wasn't improved as he headed for the dressing room when an Eagles fan taunted him from the terraces, and the volatile Frenchman responded with a flying kung fu kick, followed by a series of punches. The Frenchman was punished with an eight-month worldwide ban from all football and was stripped of the national captaincy by the French FA.

CANTONA TAKES FLIGHT

▼ Magpies Melee

http://y2u.be/4ebdYLD2_Hc

Teammates are meant to exchange passes, rather than punches, but that's exactly what happened when Newcastle United pair Kieron Dyer and Lee Bowyer came to blows during a home defeat to Aston Villa in 2009. Losing 3-0 at the time and already down to ten men, the Magpie midfielders suddenly went for each other in front of 50,000 stunned fans at St James' Park. The pair had to be pulled apart by the other players, and both were shown a red card for their troubles.

OFF THE BEATEN TRACK

North, south, east and west, there are weird and wonderful football stories everywhere – you just need to know where to look.

AN UNFORGETTABLE MATCH-UP

▲ Trunk Tactics

http://y2u.be/8g1cEliG8OM

According to legend, elephants never forget, but this jumbo duo clearly didn't remember their shin pads while playing in the annual Surin Elephant Round-Up Festival football match in Thailand. The two-day festival is all about celebrating the powerful contribution of the working elephants to the local community and, as well as the bizarre kickabout, there's also a tug-of-war between the animals and members of the Royal Thai Army.

▶ Who Ate All the Pies?

http://y2u.be/uOSGQ2ZNLV0

Sutton United made headlines in 2017 when they pulled off a huge upset, beating Leeds United to advance to the fifth round of the FA Cup.

But the National League side's dream tie with Arsenal turned into a farce thanks to substitute goalkeeper Wayne Shaw. Nicknamed the "Roly Poly Goalie" thanks to his hefty size, Shaw made a scene of digging into a pasty during the game, despite a bookmaker having offered 8-1 odds on him doing just that. An FA investigation saw him banned for two months, and he was forced to resign from Sutton.

SHAW'S NASTY PASTY

A Titan in Turkey

http://y2u.be/nXCtsxzXBKg

Former England striker Darius Vassell had a pretty successful career, racking up more than 300 appearances for Aston Villa, Manchester City and Leicester City over the years. But even he must have been shocked by the hero's welcome he received when signing for Turkish side Ankaragücü in 2009. Close to 3,000 fans turned out to cheer their team's new 'star signing', bringing flares, flags and air horns to the airport and mobbing him as he stepped off the plane. Vassell, for his part, looked pretty overwhelmed at the whole situation. Which perhaps wasn't surprising, give he'd barely played in a year and hadn't turned out for England since 2004.

▶ Messi Madness

http://y2u.be/ZjC903OGbt0

Any team in the world would love to have Argentina star Lionel Messi in their ranks and, in 2011, the deluded chairman of French village side FC Borne thought he'd try his luck and actually ask to sign the Barcelona goal machine. After one too many glasses of wine on a night out with friends, Borne's Cedric Enjolras submitted a formal request to Barca for Messi's signature, but his drunken message was intercepted by the French FA, who failed to see the funny side and immediately suspended the comedy chairman for six months.

MENIAL MISSILES

The laws of the game state that the only object that should be thrown onto the pitch is the ball – a rule which these mischievous supporters completely ignored.

RAT'S DISGUSTING!

▲ Rodent Invasion

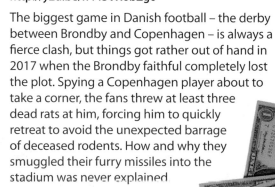

http://y2u.be/n44SVX6bZg0

The biggest game in Danish football – the derby between Brondby and Copenhagen – is always a fierce clash, but things got rather out of hand in 2017 when the Brondby faithful completely lost the plot. Spying a Copenhagen player about to take a corner, the fans threw at least three dead rats at him, forcing him to quickly retreat to avoid the unexpected barrage of deceased rodents. How and why they smuggled their furry missiles into the stadium was never explained.

Liquid Refreshment

http://y2u.be/cFmp0lw_jlo

Having a beer or two is all part of the matchday experience for many football fans, but one Bulgarian supporter had obviously had more than enough to drink during a league match between Levski Sofia and FK Vereya in 2017, throwing an unfinished can of lager onto the pitch. Remarkably, Vereya's Ivan Bandalovski decided to take a quick sip and it evidently did him the power of good, as the defender went on to score an injury-time equalizer.

◀ The Big Bang

http://y2u.be/qlRTHMA-hiM

An Iranian league game between Sepahan and Al Ahli in 2012 turned out to be an unexpectedly explosive one after someone in the crowd chucked a hand grenade onto the pitch. Footage of the game shows one of the players innocently picking up the grenade and casually throwing it toward the corner flag, only for it to go off a couple of seconds later and send two of the terrified match officials running for cover.

▶ Barcelona's Fury

http://y2u.be/kPVNolBVpn4

Signing for your club's arch rivals is a sure way to upset supporters, and Luis Figo did exactly that in 2000 when he said goodbye to Barcelona and joined Real Madrid. Two years later, he was back at the Nou Camp with his new club, and the Barcelona faithful were waiting for him, pelting the Portuguese midfielder with beer cans, lighters, bottles and golf balls whenever he got close to the touchline. Incredibly, one furious fan even lobbed a pig's head onto the pitch.

PORKY PROJECTILES

◀ Financial Windfall

http://y2u.be/N1-IZr_oNvw

Supporters hate it when star players decide to leave their beloved club, and AC Milan fans were definitely not happy when their goalkeeper, Gianluigi Donnarumma, announced in 2017 that he wouldn't be signing a new contract. They made their feelings crystal clear about his controversial decision when the teenage stopper was playing for the Italy Under-21 side at the San Siro, chucking bundles of fake dollar bills toward his goal to underline their view that Donnarumma was nothing more than a greedy traitor.

TV TERRORS

When the mics are live and the cameras start rolling, anything can happen – as these funny examples of television misfortune prove.

▶ A Stone's Throw

http://y2u.be/rwU9pHTEhA8

Venturing out of the safety of the studio to a stadium can be a risky business, and that was never more evident back in 1992 than when the BBC's *Match of the Day* set up shop at Derby's County Ground to cover the club's FA Cup clash with Swindon. All went to plan until the post-match analysis began, and a group of Swindon fans decided to pelt the window of the pundits' box inside the ground with stones.

NERVES OF STONE

TAKING EXTRA PRECAUTIONS

◀ It's Behind You!

http://y2u.be/XmGEJsynXhQ

Touchline reporters get closer than anyone to the action, but such a privileged position can sometimes be dangerous, as this German Sky Sports presenter painfully discovered at a Bundesliga match in 2014. Discussing the upcoming game as the players warmed up on the pitch, the unfortunate presenter had no idea that a stray football was about to crash into the back of her head, but viewers could see it coming from a mile off as it flew through the air toward its accidental target.

Belgian Breakage

http://y2u.be/6rosAb8CHBI

Cameras are a common sight at training grounds these days. Fans can't get enough of seeing their heroes practising their skills, and there was definitely some talent on show in 2014 as the some of the Belgium national team played a bit of keepie-up. The comedy came at the end of their game when Eden Hazard decided to hit a left-footed volley and smashed his effort straight into the lens of the camera, breaking the glass.

▲ San Siro Smash

http://y2u.be/thxRLNddnhU

Over-excited footballers can make live TV an unpredictable business, and this was never truer than when Sweden qualified for the 2018 World Cup after a play-off against Italy in the San Siro stadium in Milan. Eurosport were covering the big game and got a hell of a surprise after the final whistle, when the entire Sweden team ran across to their pitch-side reporting team and smashed up their touchline desk with their wild celebrations.

◀ Fall from Grace

http://y2u.be/368EQES_3kA

Getting the right shot is key to an eye-catching TV report and, when Sky Sports' Nick Collins was despatched to Wembley in 2013, he decided the only way to get his head and the backdrop of the stadium on camera at the same time was for him to stand on a step ladder to change the angle. His plan worked perfectly at first, but his ruse was rumbled on live TV when he slipped and hilariously fell off the ladder midway through his report.

CRAZY STADIUMS

Every team needs somewhere to play, but that doesn't mean football stadia all have to look the same, as these weird and wonderful grounds show.

Automobile Anarchy

http://y2u.be/23RQU5co-Oo

Plenty of football grounds moonlight as venues for other sports. Others even stage music concerts in their spare time, but the Schalke Arena in Germany goes even further every year when it is transformed into a Total Stock Car Racing track. It's a big job to convert the ground from football pitch to a venue for motoring madness but, with 50,000 people coming to watch the racing annually, it's probably worth all the effort.

▼ On the Water

http://y2u.be/4c4YZVpH98w

Some would argue that football's modern superstars think they can walk on water and, if they were to have a kickabout on the Float at Marina Bay in Singapore, they actually could. A pitch on a floating platform measuring 390 feet by 270 feet and weighing in at over 1,000 tonnes, the Float can hold up to 30,000 fans. It staged its first ever match in 2009 when local team Tuan Gemuk Athletic and Vietnamese side VNNTU FC played each other in a historic, waterborne fixture.

PITY THE BALLBOYS

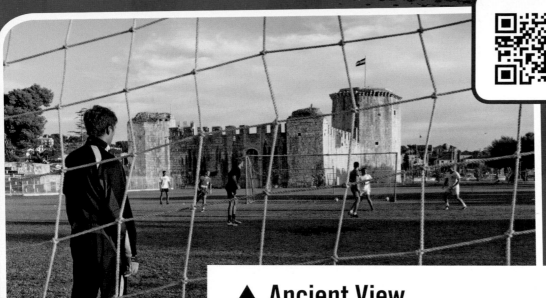

▲ Ancient View

http://y2u.be/Do9csilB-iE

The beautiful game is proud of its history, but Croatian side HNK Trogir used to enjoy an even older connection with the past when they played their home games at the Igraliste Batarija Stadium. The ground itself wasn't that old, but the fifteenth-century castle at one end of the pitch definitely was and certainly made for an unusual backdrop to a match. Sadly, Trogir folded in 2009 but, while the club is no more, the castle is most definitely still standing.

A PITCH WITH A VIEW

▶ Retractable Pitch

http://y2u.be/V3i_Dtz9dhM

A good slide tackle can be a thing of beauty, but it's the entire pitch inside the Sapporo Dome in Japan, rather than the players, that does the sliding. Built for the 2002 World Cup, the stadium boasts a retractable 8,300-tonne pitch, which can be moved in and out of the dome to expose the turf to sunlight when the weather is good and can also be rotated 90 degrees to improve the view for spectators, depending whether the ground is staging football or baseball.

▶ Magical Marta

http://y2u.be/UZywdRNArnw

Marta Vieira da Silva went in to the 2007 FIFA
Women's World Cup in China as the reigning
FIFA Women's World Player of the Year, so
expectations were high. She met them – and
then some, shrugging off the pressure to
produce a series of sublime performances,
leading Brazil all the way to the final. Arguably
the best goal of Marta's glittering career also
came in this tournament against the United
States – a stunning strike that showcased her
close control, ball trickery and lethal finishing.
It's no wonder that the media have nicknamed
Marta "Pele in a skirt".

THE CRAZY GANG

Every profession and walk of life has its fair share of mavericks and eccentrics, and the beautiful game is no exception to the rule.

▶ Alien Invasion

http://y2u.be/1w2dMekIJLw

There was nothing at all unusual about David Icke's brief career as a goalkeeper with Coventry and Hereford United, but what happened next was truly unbelievable. Forced to retire due to arthritis at the age of 21, Icke forged a career as a TV sports presenter but went spectacularly off the rails when he became interested in New Age philosophies and, in 1991, he publicly predicted the world would end in six years' time. He later declared himself the son of God, before saying that Earth was secretly ruled by a race of reptile-like aliens.

▼ Twitter Pioneer

http://y2u.be/Hka4NLtA3o4

Colourful and always controversial, English midfielder Joey Barton has never been a stereotypical footballer. Once jailed for assault and affray, Barton showed his softer side when he began writing a column for homeless magazine *The Big Issue* and also fronted the "Get Hooked on Fishing" campaign. It was, however, his contribution to Twitter that truly marked him out as an eccentric, with Barton declining to tell the world what he was having for tea and, instead, using the social-media platform to quote the likes of Friedrich Nietzsche, George Orwell, Isambard Kingdom Brunel and even famously miserable Manchester singer, Morrissey.

Geography Lesson

http://y2u.be/W3EA4NqiaNM

Nicknamed "Drillo", Norwegian Egil Olsen has never been a typical manager and, although Wimbledon fans during the 1999–2000 season will never forget him wearing Wellington boots on the touchline, his unusual choice of footwear was merely the tip of the iceberg. A member of the Norwegian Workers' Communist Party, Olsen was also famed for memorizing the height of every mountain on the planet and was so obsessed with geographical trivia that he wrote a 2002 book entitled *Drillo's World*, which sadly failed to trouble the Norwegian Top 10 best-sellers list.

Animal Magic

http://y2u.be/_08YpwxWlcg

Plenty of players are superstitious, but Senegalese midfielder Papa Bouba Diop took it to a whole new level in 2004 when he was a Fulham player. The Cottagers were hovering nervously above the relegation places so Diop decided to perform a tradition "ju-ju" ritual (a kind of West African voodoo) at Craven Cottage to change the team's luck, sprinkling animal blood over the pitch. The groundsman was furious, but the magical intervention seemed to work and Fulham finished the season safely in 13th place.

▼ Loony Lehmann

http://y2u.be/Se2h0GCMozA

It's fair to say that Germany goalkeeper Jens Lehmann never exactly played by the rules during a controversial career, and his list of unorthodox misdemeanours is longer than one of his goal kicks. Throwing an opponent's boot into the crowd, ripping off another's headband, stealing a supporter's glasses and pouring water over a referee all raised more than a few eyebrows, but he really joined the game's eccentric elite when he "relieved" himself behind an advertising hoarding during a 2009 Champions League clash between Stuttgart and Unirea Urziceni.

MEDIA MADNESS

These comedy press conference moments prove that the beautiful game, and those who play it, definitely have a sense of humour.

Forty Winks

http://y2u.be/OPe63DTnj24

Managers of top teams are used to dealing with the world's media, but Real Madrid boss Luis Enrique was completely thrown off balance in 2017 when he spotted a journalist sleeping in one of his press conferences. The Spaniard initially found the sleepy reporter funny but became more and more annoyed by his inattention, and then had to grit his teeth as the tired writer woke up and decided to leave the room altogether.

▼ ZZ's Shower

http://y2u.be/2iqHBjSLlTI

Real Madrid boss Zinedine Zidane was all smiles after his team had beaten Sevilla to lift the UEFA Super Cup in Norway in 2016 and, surprisingly, he was still laughing even after his own players attacked him in the post-match press conference. The Frenchman was talking to the assembled media when half of his over-excited team gatecrashed the party, storming uninvited onto the stage where Zidane was sat and soaking the gaffer with their numerous water bottles.

A PRESS CONFERENCE SOAKING

▼ World Cup Confusion

http://y2u.be/62fe_B7mUu4

Some cynics say the USA just doesn't understand football, and one American journalist rather added to the argument during a 2016 press conference. The media were there to speak to German legend Bastian Schweinsteiger, who had just signed for MLS side Chicago Fire from Man United, when our misinformed reporter asked the midfielder whether he thought the team could potentially win the World Cup. Much confusion followed until one of the Chicago staff finally pointed out that only international teams, and not club sides, played in the competition.

▶ It's for You!

http://y2u.be/VVX6jdDRyWI

Journalists interrupt managers at their peril, and a talkSPORT reporter must have feared the worst in 2017 when he accidentally stopped Man United boss Jose Mourinho in full flow. The red-faced journalist had left his phone in front of the Portuguese coach to record his press conference but was mortified when the mobile rang, forcing Mourinho to stop talking, pick up the mobile and answer the call. Luckily for him, the United manager saw the funny side.

"CAN I TAKE A MESSAGE?"

ANGER MANAGEMENT

Football is a passionate game, but sometimes players and match officials cross the line when they completely lose the plot.

Crazy Kadyrov

http://y2u.be/jv9S_qw8zFU

Exactly what youngster Ilya Krichmara said to linesman Musa Kadyrov during a junior match in Russia between Amkar and Terek in 2013 is a mystery, but it definitely got a reaction from the assistant referee. In fact, he went absolutely ballistic, dropping his flag and grabbing Krichmara by the throat, pushing the teenager down onto the grass and then repeatedly kicking him. Unsurprisingly, the Russian FA took a dim view of his assault, fining Kadyrov £10,000 and banning him from the touchline for life.

▼ Pepe's Red Mist descends

http://y2u.be/Ec0CT8yzjAo

Real Madrid's game with Getafe back in 2009 was a tasty one, but that was still no excuse for Pepe's incredible attack on Javi Casquero. The Getafe midfielder broke into the box but was pushed over by the Portuguese defender. Casquero, however, didn't even have time to scream for a penalty, as Pepe first slammed his right boot smack into his shins and then aimed another swinging boot and raked his studs all the way down Casquero's back. It surprised absolutely no one when the Madrid man was promptly sent off.

PEPE, CALM AS EVER

Feeble Fight

http://y2u.be/nLQubgk9EkY

It's usually the hardest players who finds themselves in the middle of a fight, but Sevilla's Luis Fabiano and Real Zaragoza's Carlos Diogo were the exception to the rule in 2007, with one of the game's most pathetic and hilarious dust-ups ever. The angry duo's attempts to punch each other were pure comedy, as they weaved their arms around without making any real contact. That said, their antics still landed them in hot water when the referee managed to stop laughing and booked them both.

▼ Ball-boy Bully

http://y2u.be/sd38KUjmOho

There was uproar in England in 2013 when Chelsea's Eden Hazard had a moment of utter madness during a League Cup clash with Swansea City. The Belgian star was rather to keen to retrieve the ball, but one of the Swans' ball boys decided to lie on top of it to delay him, and Hazard reacted by giving the lad a sly kick in the ribs. It wasn't sly enough, though, and he was given a three-match ban for violent conduct.

No Place Like Home

Football stadia come in many different shapes and sizes but some, as these examples prove, really have to be seen to believe.

▼ Colour Co-ordinated

http://y2u.be/w4PSlfJYKm8

Football's answer to the chameleon, the Allianz Arena in Germany, is home to club sides Bayern Munich and 1860 München, and the ground's designers came up with the clever idea to make both teams feel at home with an ingenious lighting system on the outside of the stadium. So, when Bayern play, the LED panels turn red, but the ground becomes blue when 1860 have a fixture. The Allianz can even be transformed into white when the German national team is in town.

Head for Heights

http://y2u.be/Gr9BPKABAj0

Ottmar Hitzfeld Stadium is home to Swiss side FC Gspon, while the tiny club is hardly one of football's heavyweights, it proudly boasts the highest ground anywhere in Europe. Nestled in the Alps near the ski resort of Zermatt, the pitch is 2,000 metres above sea level and is the only place for miles flat enough to play a game. The big problem for FC Gspon is the cost of buying new balls, losing, on average, seven every match when they're kicked over the protective netting and disappear down the mountain.

▲ Green Agenda

http://y2u.be/dFt-pYVPVp4

The grass is usually the greenest thing inside a football stadium, but the Estadio Janguito Malucelli in Brazil is an interesting exception to the rule. Not a single drop of concrete or an ounce of metal was used in the construction of the ground, earning the unusual venue the nickname of the "Brazil Eco-Stadium". The main stand was built on a hill, with the seating cut out of the earth, and only recycled wood was used for the changing rooms and other buildings.

▽ Rock and a Hard Place

http://y2u.be/P5FVyj2dL3A

It cost £70 million to build the Estádio Municipal de Braga in Portugal for the 2004 European Championships, and the big price tag is hardly surprising when you realize the constructors had to shift millions of tonnes of solid rock to build the stadium. With a capacity of just over 30,000, the ground is nestled in an old, abandoned quarry and, behind one of the goals, there is an eye-catching wall of natural stone, rather than the usual rows of seating.

BRAGA'S STADIUM ROCKS

THE ANIMAL KINGDOM

Playing in the great outdoors inevitably means that, sooner or later, football has to contend with some unexpected and uninvited guests.

▼ Fowl Play

http://y2u.be/EnqyBpSCWJQ

Blackburn fans weren't exactly over the moon in 2010 when their club was bought by the Venky family – the owners of an Indian poultry company – and the Rovers faithful decided to demonstrate their disapproval at Ewood Park a couple of years later by releasing a chicken onto the pitch, causing a bit of a stir as the bird strutted around behind the goal. Blackburn, sadly, were still relegated that season, while the fate of the poor chicken remains a mystery.

CHICKEN, RUN!

▶ Insect Invasion

http://y2u.be/M2QV6L5oDMs

It's not uncommon for an overexcited fan to run onto the pitch to congratulate a player who's just scored a goal, but it's very unusual for a giant grasshopper to join the celebrations. That, though, is just what happened in the 2014 World Cup quarter-final clash between Colombia and Brazil when James Rodriguez scored from the penalty spot. The Colombian ran back to the centre circle, blissfully unaware he was now giving a piggyback to a massive grasshopper clinging to his right arm.

JAMES'
HITCHHIKER

▼ Back from the Dead

http://y2u.be/dFt-pYVPVp4

Seagulls are repeat offenders when it comes to invading sporting events, and one of them nearly paid a heavy price when it got in the way of the ball as Sydney FC took on Melbourne in 2016. The pass seemed to have killed the bird and it was absolutely lifeless as Sydney FC goalkeeper Danny Vukovic carried the body over to the touchline. The match restarted, but there was a happy ending when, a few minutes later, the cameras spotted the gull alive and well, sitting on the Sydney bench.

▼ Making a Bee-line

http://y2u.be/lWv55gjb61Q

Everybody knows about the dangers of an angry bee, but the players of Ponte Preta and Atletico Sorocaba in Brazil had a whole swarm of them to worry about in 2013. The swarm decided it rather liked the look of one of the goals inside the Estádio Moisés Lucarelli, setting up home, en masse, on the crossbar. Before the game could start, the uninvited insect invaders had to be smoked out.

153

BONKERS BALL BOYS

Collecting stray balls should be a straightforward job, but sometimes ball boys just can't help putting themselves in the spotlight.

Below the Belt

http://y2u.be/-gUgPkJ76x8

One of football's golden – if cruellest – rules is: should a player get hit by the ball in the groin, the crowd must laugh long and loud at their painful misfortune. The fans at White Hart Lane for Tottenham's Europa League clash with Cypriot side Famagusta were, therefore, in absolute stitches when one of the ball boys chucked the ball to an opposition player but got the trajectory of his throw a little off and only succeeded in hitting him where it hurts.

▼ Harsh Head Throw

http://y2u.be/5V6SQ0AYoR0

The whole point of ball boys is to get the football back to the players as quickly as possible, so it was perfectly understandable that FC Tubize goalkeeper Quentin Beunardeau was annoyed when he had to fetch the ball himself from behind the goal in a Belgian league game in 2016. It was less understandable, when Beunardeau had finally got his hands on it, that he took out his frustration by chucking the football at the nearest ball boy's head.

Rapid Reaction

http://y2u.be/FOn8ISMMLZo

Ball boys need to be keen, but the South African youngster charged with retrieving footballs during the Kaiser Chiefs' fixture with Cape Town in 2016 was a little too eager. An injury-time Chiefs attack saw the ball fired across the face of goal and the lad obviously thought it was going out for a goal kick and quickly threw another ball onto the pitch. Unfortunately, the other ball stayed in play, and the referee was so angry with the innocent mistake that he sent the young chap to the stands in disgrace.

Pet Rescue

http://y2u.be/s-OB4I0i_rs

A Bolivian league game descended into chaos in 2014 when a trio of stray dogs ran onto the pitch. The canine intruders ran amok until one of the players grabbed one of the pooches and tried to carry it off. The problem was that the player was rather rough with the dog, repeatedly dropping the pitch invader as he manhandled it, and it was only when a kind-hearted ball boy stepped in and told him to lay off the poor pooch that it was able to escape without any further damage.

◀ One-Nil to the Ball Boy

http://y2u.be/U-PF8FpiJTA

Superstar footballers aren't used to being made fools of but a cheeky Atletico Madrid ball boy made a right mug out of Cristiano Ronaldo in 2014 in the city derby against Real Madrid. Ronaldo was in a mood because he wanted to take a quick throw-in, and he gestured angrily to the lad, who shrugged his shoulders in reply. The Madrid forward then went running over to the youngster, who Ronaldo think he was going to give him the ball. However, at the last second, the ball boy threw it away, leaving an embarrassed Ronaldo standing there like an idiot.

Touchline Prankster

http://y2u.be/8zQEyajHoKs

The ball boy at QPR's clash with Aston Villa in 2015 obviously fancied himself as a bit of a joker, although he definitely didn't intend the first laugh in this clip. Racing to retrieve the ball, he embarrassingly fell over on the slippery surface but, once he was back on his feet, he had the crowd in stitches as he teased QPR keeper Robert Green with a series of fake throw backs before nutmegging the former England stopper.

BEHIND THE SCENES

Team dressing rooms used to be private places but, with cameras everywhere these days, we can now see exactly what happens behind closed doors.

▼ Champions at War

http://y2u.be/RIknXzE3OoQ

The PSG dressing room should have been a happy place in 2013 after the club had just clinched the French league title, but the camera that was allowed access to the "celebrations" actually captured a blazing row. The argument was between star striker Zlatan Ibrahimovic and Brazilian Leonardo, the club's director of football, and, while everyone else was clearly in party mood, the feuding pair had a verbal spat that rather spoiled the atmosphere. Perhaps, coincidentally, Leonardo quit the club a couple of months later.

ZLATAN VS LEO: THERE COULD ONLY BE ONE WINNER

JOE
HAD HIS
TEAMMATES
IN STITCHES

▲ Ledley the Lunatic

http://y2u.be/_haTdoIbQRw

Wales enjoyed a brilliant Euro 2016, going all the way to the semi-finals, but the highlight of the tournament could be Joe Ledley's absolutely insane dressing-room dance routine. Filmed after Wales had beaten Northern Ireland in Paris in the Last 16, the madcap midfielder jumped up to entertain his teammates with a series of hilarious moves, finishing off his show with a potentially career-ending dive along the table. It was both brilliant and bizarre all at the same time.

▶ Bin Men

http://y2u.be/cRqG-8h7DCQ

The Syracuse soccer team in the USA were obviously in ambitious mood after a game in 2016 and, rather than a quick shower and heading home, they decided to take on the bin challenge. With 25 players seated around one youngster in the middle, they attempted to go around the whole circle heading the ball back and forth before finally nodding it into a bin in the middle of the dressing room. Impressively, the lads pulled it off and went absolutely mental when the ball finally hit its target.

INDEX

PICTURE CREDITS

The publishers would like to thank the following sources for their kind permission to reproduce the pictures in this book.

4 Jean Catuffe/Getty Images, 5 Maxisport/Shutterstock, 7 Bob Thomas/Getty Images, 8 (top) Andrew Yates/AFP/Getty Images, (bottom) Fredrik Sandberg/AFP/Getty Images, 9 (top) Popperfoto/Getty Images, (bottom) Michael Steele/Getty Images, 10 (bottom) Stephane de Sakutin/AFP/Getty Images, 11 (top) Gualter Fatia/Getty Images, (bottom) TF-Images/Getty Images, 12 (left) Benjawan Sermkietsakul/Shutterstock, (right) Paul Ellis/AFP/Getty Images, 13 (top) Matthew Ashton/AMA/Corbis/Getty Images, (bottom) Jasper Juinen/Getty Images, 14-15 (bottom) Gerardo Zavala/LatinContent/Getty Images, 15 (top) Denis Doyle/Getty Images, 16 Matthew Ashton/AMA/Corbis/Getty Images, 17 (top) Eric Vandeville/Gamma-Rapho/Getty Images, (bottom) Zhang Peng/LightRocket/Getty Images, 18 (top) Shutterstock, (bottom) Kitch Bain/Shutterstock, 19 (top) AGIF/Shutterstock, (bottom) Pete Norton/Getty Images, 20 (top) AFP/Getty Images, (bottom) Tony McArdle/Everton FC/Getty Images, 21 Angel Martinez/Real Madrid CF/Getty Images, 22 Photomaster/Shutterstock, 23 (top) Alex Caparros/Getty Images, (bottom) Dziurek/Shutterstock, 24-25 VI Images/Getty Images, 24 (left) Chris Harvey/Shutterstock, 25 (right) Martin Rose/Bongarts/Getty Images, 26 AFP/Getty Images, 27 (top) Foc Kan/GC Images/Getty Images, (bottom) VI Images/Getty Images, 28 Bob Thomas/Getty Images, 29 (left) Alex Livesey/Getty Images, (right) Christof Koepsel/Bongarts/Getty Images, 30 (left) oneinchpunch/Shutterstock, (right) Filippo Monteforte/AFP/Getty Images, 31 (top) Denis Doyle/Getty Images, (bottom) Mark Leech/Offside/Getty Images, 32 Richard Heathcote/Getty Images, 33 Bob Thomas/Getty Images, 34 VI Images/Getty Images, 35 (top) Laurence Griffiths/Getty Images, (bottom) Oli Scarff/AFP/Getty Images, 36 Michael Steele/Getty Images, 37 (top) Anders Wiklund/AFP/Getty Images, (bottom) Alex Livesey/Getty Images, 38 (top) fstockfoto/Shutterstock, (bottom) LongJon/Shutterstock, 39 (top) Shaun Botterill/Getty Images, (bottom) Samo Vidic/Getty Images, 40 Carmen Wagner/LatinContent/Getty Images, 41 (top) AFP/Getty Images, (bottom) Matthew Ashton/AMA/Corbis/Getty Images, 42-43 Daniel Smith/Warner Bros./Kobal/REX/Shutterstock, 44 Ljupco Smokovski/Shutterstock, 45 Allsport/Getty Images, 46 Matthew Ashton/AMA/Corbis/Getty Images, 47 (top) Dreamstime, (bottom) sirtravelalot/Shutterstock, 48-49 Laurence Griffiths/Getty Images, 48 (top) urbanbuzz/Shutterstock, 49 (top) SOMKKU/Shutterstock, 50 (left) Ian Horrocks/Newcastle United FC/Getty Images, (right) Ross Kinnaird/Getty Images, 51 (top) Andrew Yates/AFP/Getty Images, (bottom) Stu Forster/Getty Images, 52 Georges Gobet/AFP/Getty Images, 53 Eugene Onischenko/Shutterstock, 54 Jacopo Raule/Getty Images, 55 (top) Fabrice Coffrini/AFP/Getty Images, (bottom) Popperfoto/Getty Images, 56 (left) canbedone/Shutterstock, (right) Mustafa Ozer/AFP/Getty Images, 57 (top) pixelschoen/Shutterstock, (centre) Sean Gallup/Getty Images, (bottom) Bob Thomas/Getty Images, 58-59 Odd Andersen/AFP/Getty Images, 60 (left) David Cannon/Getty Images, (right) Brendon Thorne/Getty Images, 61 Popperfoto/Getty Images, 62 (top) Tom Purslow/Manchester United FC/Getty Images, (bottom) iodrakon/Shutterstock, 63 (top) Andrew Yates/AFP/Getty Images, (bottom) andreaciox/Shutterstock, 64 (top) Andreas Rentz/Bongarts/Getty Images, (bottom) marcokenya/Shutterstock, 65 (top) G Gershoff/WireImage/Getty Images, (bottom) Eric Renard/Corbis/Getty Images, 66 Pierre-Philippe Marcou/AFP/Getty Images, 67 (top) Giuseppe Cacace/AFP/Getty Images, (bottom) Shaun Botterill/Getty Images, 68 (top) Savo Prelevic/AFP/Getty Images, (bottom) Marilyn Barbone/Shutterstock, 69 (left) Sukpaiboonwat/Shutterstock, (right) Jean Catuffe/Getty Images, 70 (left) Ljupco Smokovski/Shutterstock, (right) Valery Hache/AFP/Getty Images, 71 (top) Roberto Schmidt/AFP/Getty Images, (bottom) Gerard Julien/AFP/Getty Images, 72 Paul Ellis/AFP/Getty Images, 73 (top) Mike Hewitt/Getty Images, (bottom) picturepartners/Shutterstock, 74 (top) Popperfoto/Getty Images, (bottom) Ayman alakhras/Shutterstock, 75 (top) Tom Jenkins/Getty Images, (bottom) Yves Boucau/AFP/Getty Images, 76 (top) Christian Bertrand/Shutterstock, (bottom) Ievgenii Meyer/Shutterstock, 77 (top) ninikas/Shutterstock, (bottom) Alex Livesey/FIFA/Getty Images, 78 (top) Gary M Prior/Allsport/Getty Images, 78-79 (bottom) Martin Meissner/REX/Shutterstock, 80 (left) Miguel Medina/AFP/Getty Images, (right) Bob Thomas/Getty Images, 81 (top) Matthew Ashton/AMA/Corbis/Getty Images, (bottom) Alberto Pizzoli/AFP/Getty Images, 82 Getty Images, 83 Ben Stansall/AFP/Getty Images, 84-85 Adek Berry/AFP/Getty Images, 86 Alexander Ishchenko/Shutterstock, 86-87 Lars Baron/Getty Images, 88 Lefty Shivambu/Gallo Images/Getty Images, 89 (top) Lars Baron/Getty Images, (right) Tita77/Shutterstock, (bottom) Imago/REX/Shutterstock, 90 Anthony Wallace/AFP/Getty Images, 91 Miguel Medina/AFP/Getty Images, 92 Ali Burafi/AFP/Getty Images, 93 Martin Bureau/AFP/Getty Images, 94 Michal Cizek/AFP/Getty Images, 95 Jan Kruger/Getty Images, 96 Stuart MacFarlane/Arsenal FC/Getty Images, 97 (left) Vincent van Doornick/Isosport/MB Media/Getty Images, (right) Filipe Frazao/Shutterstock, 98 Bob Thomas/Getty Images, 99 (top) Laurent Zabulon/Gamma-Rapho/Getty Images, (bottom) Joern Pollex/Getty Images, 100 Mike Hewitt/Getty Images, 101 (top) Vagelis Georgariou/ActionPlus/Corbis/Getty Images, (bottom) Tatiana Popova/Shutterstock, 102 (top) Peter Bischoff/Getty Images, (bottom) Dave Hogan/Getty Images, 103 (top) Ziviani/Shutterstock, (bottom) Allsport/Getty Images, 104-105 Boris Streubel/Getty Images, 106 Kevork Djansezian/Getty Images, 107 (top) AFP/Getty Images, (bottom) Lars Baron/Bongarts/Getty Images, 108 Joern Pollex/Getty Images, 109 (top) Simon Hofmann/Bongarts/Getty Images, (centre) Darren Walsh/Chelsea FC/Getty Images, (bottom) Salamahin/Shutterstock, 110 E.O./Shutterstock, 111 (top) Andrew Powell/Liverpool FC/Getty Images, (bottom) Gavin Morrison/Shutterstock, 112 (top) Dave Hogan/Getty Images, (bottom) David Cannon/Getty Images, 113 (top) Ulf Wittrock/Shutterstock, (bottom) Popperfoto/Getty Images, 114 (left) Alan Rennie/Action Plus/Getty Images, (right) James Baylis/AMA/Corbis/Getty Images, 115 Tullio M Puglia/Getty Images, 116 Stuart Franklin/FIFA/Getty Images, 117 Ljupco Smokovski/Shutterstock, 118 (left) Anatolii Riepin/Shutterstock, (right) Shaun Botterill/Getty Images, 119 (top) Michael Dechev/Shutterstock, (bottom) Mark Leech/Offside/Getty Images, 120 (top) Ben Radford/Getty Images, (bottom) David Cannon/Getty Images, 121 (top) Ben Radford/Getty Images, (bottom) Bob Thomas/Getty Images, 122 Paul Drinkwater/NBCU Photo Bank/Getty Images, 123 Paul Gilham/Getty Images, 124 Oleh Dubyna/Shutterstock, 125 (top) exopixel/Shutterstock, (bottom) ConstantinosZ/Shutterstock, 126-127 Issouf Sanogo/AFP/Getty Images, 128 Chadakorn Phalanon/Shutterstock, 129 Paul Bergstrom/Icon Sportswire/Corbis/Getty Images, 130 Luis Acosta/AFP/Getty Images, 131 (top) Alicia Chelini/Shutterstock, (bottom) NurPhoto/Getty Images, 132-133 John MacDougall/AFP/Getty Images, 133 (top) ActionPlus/Corbis/Getty Images, (bottom) Laurence Griffiths/Getty Images, 134 AFP/Getty Images, 135 (top) Joe Gough/Shutterstock, (bottom) Maxisport/Shutterstock, 136 Lars Ronbog/FrontZoneSport/Getty Images, 137 (top) Rob Byron/Shutterstock, (right) Firo Foto/Getty Images, (bottom) Dalibor Sevaljevic/Shutterstock, 138 (top) Palii Oleg/Shutterstock, (bottom) Alex Grimm/Bongarts/Getty Images, 139 (top) Nils Petter Nilsson/Getty Images, (bottom) Ewa Studio/Shutterstock, 140 Comaniciu Dan/Shutterstock, 141 (top) Henryk T Kaiser/Photolibrary/Getty Images, (bottom) tkyszk/Shutterstock, 142-143 Simon Bruty/Sports Illustrated/Getty Images, 144 (top) Colin Davey/Getty Images, (bottom) MSPT/Shutterstock, 145 Phil Cole/Getty Images, 146 Antonio Villalba/Real Madrid CF/Getty Images, 147 (top) Lev Radin/Shutterstock, (bottom) John Peters/Manchester United FC/Getty Images, 148 Miguel Riopa/AFP/Getty Images, 149 Michael Steele/Getty Images, 150 Lennart Preiss/Bongarts/Getty Images, 151 (top) Kirill Kudryavtsev/AFP/Getty Images, (bottom) Bruno Pires/EuroFootball/Getty Images, 152 Andrew Yates/AFP/Getty Images, 153 (top) Eric Isselee/Shutterstock, (bottom left) s_oleg/Shutterstock, (bottom right) Peter Waters/Shutterstock, 154 Guillaume Souvant/AFP/Getty Images, 154-155 Francesc Juan/Shutterstock, 156 Marc Piasecki/WireImage/Getty Images, 157 (top) Stu Forster/Getty Images, (bottom) Quality Stock Arts/Shutterstock

Every effort has been made to acknowledge correctly and contact the source and/or copyright holder of each picture and Carlton Books Limited apologises for any unintentional errors or omissions, which will be corrected in future editions of this book.